ABOVE THE CLOUDS

Memoirs of a B-26 Marauder Pilot

Major Richard M. Crummett
(USAF, Retired)

Copyright © 2011 by Richard M. Crummett

First Edition – July 2011

Edited by Cheryl Crummett.

Cover photo: B-26 Marauder, pre-flight inspection by Lt. Crummett, May, 1944 at Rivenhall, England.

ISBN

978-1-77067-291-8 (Hardcover)

978-1-77067-292-5 (Paperback)

978-1-77067-293-2 (eBook)

All rights reserved.

No part of this publication may be reproduced in any form, or by any means, electronic or mechanical, including photocopying, recording, or any information browsing, storage, or retrieval system, without permission in writing from the publisher.

Published by:

FriesenPress

Suite 300 – 852 Fort Street

Victoria, BC, Canada V8W 1H8

www.friesenpress.com

Distributed to the trade by The Ingram Book Company

Table of Contents

Prologue: History of the B-26 Marauder ix
Chapter 1: Youthful Inspiration 1
Chapter 2: Choices and Anticipation 3
Chapter 3: Air Corps Initiation 7
Chapter 4: Aviation Cadets 11
Chapter 5: Introduction to the Marauder:
               Love at First Sight 15
Chapter 6: Getting to the Fight 19
Chapter 7: Preparation for Combat 25
Chapter 8: Engaging the Enemy 29
Chapter 9: Busting Bridges 37
Chapter 10: Rest and Relaxation 41
Chapter 11: Hammering the Nazis 47
Chapter 12: A-26 Field, Normandy:
               Onward into France 51
Chapter 13: A-41 Field, Dreux:
               50th Mission R and R 57
Chapter 14: A-72 Field, Mons en Chasse:
               Getting to Know the French 61
Chapter 15: I am First Pilot with My Own Crew:
               Bombing the German Homeland 67
Chapter 16: Rescuing the Boys at the Bulge:
               The Beginning of the End 71
Chapter 17: My First Dead-Stick Landing 75
Chapter 18: My Second Dead-Stick Landing 81
Chapter 19: Nightmarish Practical Joke 87
Chapter 20: A Bout with Anoxia 89

Chapter 21: 1st Army Adventure 93
Chapter 22: Dangerous Liaisons 101
Chapter 23: Y-55 Field, Venlo, Holland:
          My Nightmare 105
Chapter 24: The War in Europe Ends:
          Going Home 109
Epilogue 113
Awards 121
First Crew 122
Second Crew 123
Acknowledgement 124
Valhalla 125

High Flight

Oh! I have slipped the surly bonds of Earth
And danced the skies on laughter-silvered wings;
Sunward I've climbed, and joined the tumbling mirth
Of sun-split clouds, — and done a hundred things
You have not dreamed of — wheeled and soared and swung
High in the sunlit silence. Hov'ring there,
I've chased the shouting wind along, and flung
My eager craft through footless halls of air . . .

Up, up the long, delirious burning blue
I've topped the wind-swept heights with easy grace
Where never lark, or ever eagle flew —
And, while with silent, lifting mind I've trod
The high untrespassed sanctity of space,
Put out my hand, and touched the face of God.

— John Gillespie Magee, Jr.

Dedication

I dedicate this book to my wife, Jane Catherine (Wolan) Crummett; the most precious lady I have ever known. She has been the most sincere, virtuous, forthright, loving, compassionate and faithful partner a man could want. I love and owe so much to this girl; may God eventually bless her fully. She's been most considerate and patient, supporting my efforts to pass on my combat experiences.

Prologue

History of the B-26 Marauder

In the late 1930's, President Roosevelt began to realize that war was likely to happen in Europe. He knew that we were totally unprepared, in the event that we may have to enter into the conflict. By 1939, he had figured how to sell some arms and airplanes to the British and French. After the war began in Europe, it became apparent that air power was a decisive factor. We were producing a P-40 fighter and a B-17 heavy bomber, which the British said were not quite good enough. They needed more development and improved performance. We were making a light bomber, similar to our B-20 and the British found them adequate.

The President notified the war plane companies that he wanted thousands of planes—fighters and bombers. Specifications were put out for a medium bomber in March of 1939. They called for a high speed medium bomber, speed 250-350 mph, range of 3,000 miles, capable of 20,000-30,000' ceiling, carrying a bomb load of

3,000 lbs., with 4 – 30 caliber guns. Production from drawings was allowed, with no prototype testing.

Five companies submitted proposals; Martin's Magruder design team's model #179 received the highest score. In September of 1939, Martin was given an order for 201 copies of this bomber. The plane was named the Marauder; the Air Corps called it the B-26. It was designed to have the speed and maneuverability of a fighter, while having a heavy bomber's bomb capacity. Although new tooling and equipment had to be built, production procedures had to be established and the plant had to be expanded to accommodate this new work, he began to make B-26's.

By the fall of 1940, he had received two additional contracts for over 1,000 planes. He started building a new plant in November and by April, workers were putting together Marauders there. The first B-26 rolled out of the plant on 25December 1940. Martin's test pilot flew it on 30December 1940. The Air Corps came and took four planes. They began 113-hour test flight trials. The Air Corps completed the tests and accepted the planes in February of 1941. They found the top speed to be 315 mph and landing speed was 130 mph—pretty hot!

B-26 Marauder. Taken at A-72 Field, Mons en Chasse, France, October, 1944

The flight trials revealed that the weight-carrying capabilities of the B-26 was about a ton more than the original design specifications. This allowed an increase of the bomb load and the possibility to add beneficial equipment. With this maximum load, they could get airborne in 2,500' of runway.

The first contract planes went to an old regular Air Corps unit. These pilots, crews, maintenance and support people had many years of experience. They handled any problem that (rarely) arose, without any trouble. They fought the Japanese from Australia and Alaska in 1942, They engaged in dog-fights with the Jap Zero; they claimed to have shot down 13 fighters, while losing only seven B-26's.

Soon, back in the U.S., there were worrisome accidents occurring at the training units teaching new pilots to fly the B-26's. The politicians thought of abolishing the B-26 production. The top Air Corps generals told them the plane had an excellent combat record, and the problem was something other than the plane.

Investigation revealed two major causes. First, the new pilots graduating from the aviation cadet flight training schools were not prepared for this high performance aircraft. The shift from a slow, docile, low-powered plane with 200 hp engines, to a super-performance 2,000 hp high speed racing monster was too big a step for some. There should have been a faster, more difficult to fly, higher powered plane with at least 1,000 hp in between to prepare them. Eventually, they used the B-25's, which are much easier to fly and are lighter and slower.

Next, they found that the training of the new mechanics and flight engineers did not include the proper higher technology electrical instruction required to service, inspect and repair the B-26. Also, they found many problems came from a lack of consideration for the normal center of gravity of the designers, which was established for a fully equipped plane, carrying a full crew with a maximum combat load of bombs and ammunition.

Martin was quick in making changes as required, to insure his plane was sturdy and safe to fly. The pilots loved the initially produced planes. They had de-icer boots on the wings, de-icer systems for the cockpit windows, oxygen for high altitudes, a fixed emergency generator for starting and pre-flighting planes and a chemical toilet for maximum (10-hour plus) range flights. Soon, all these necessary items were eliminated. Many pilots died because of the lack of these "unnecessary convenient luxuries."

The large internal space, plus its capacity to carry a greater load, soon resulted in lots of additional equipment added, including armor plates. To maintain Martin's desired margin of safety, the wingspan was increased, as was the span of the horizontal stabilizer-elevator assembly and the rudder was enlarged. This required more powerful engines. The end result was a slower medium bomber, which was less like a fighter plane.

This super performance, fast, heavy bomb-load capability, higher technology, extremely strong and sturdy plane was chosen for the European Theatre of Operations. Apparently because they thought it could stand up to the superior antiaircraft defenses of the Nazi war machine better than any other plane.

When the ETO war ended, the B-26's combat losses for the number of combat sorties flown was three tenths of one percent, (the lowest of all the planes in that war of WWII).

Probably this was possible because Martin's Magruder engineering team designed and incorporated advanced higher technology equipment into the Marauder. The propellers with four blades, 13.5' diameter, electrically controlled, full featuring, and constant-speed type were a first. Also, a first was the electric-powered, twin 50 caliber, full 360 degree swiveling armored top turret gun. This was made and sold to other plane manufacturers later. The twin 50 caliber electric-powered armored tail gun, (where the gunner fired while sitting) was unique. The gas tanks were the first to have the Martin-developed, self-sealing "mareng" linings to prevent leaks. These were also sold to other plane manufacturers later.

In summary, from 1941 through 1944, the B-26 Marauder was the fastest, strongest, most rugged medium bomber, carrying the heaviest bomb load in the world.

Chapter 1

Youthful Inspiration

I was born 25May1922 in Clinton, Maine, on a dairy farm, the second child with one brother and five sisters. When I was 6 years old, my father took me to a field near Benton to an air-show. This was put on by some barnstormers flying WWI biplanes, and I fell in love with planes and becoming a pilot right then. I started working at around 8 years old and attended a one-room school-house in Morrison's Corner. I did chores in the barn and helped to deliver milk on the milk route visiting cousins and uncles on the way. They always saved their magazines for me since they knew I loved to read; especially those stories about the Great War (WWI).

Both Grandfather and Father were skilled woodsmen. They taught me how to fish, hunt and trap. By age 13, I owned my first rifle and could shoot a 45 revolver. I learned compassion and courage from my paternal Grandmother, who was part Indian, and Grandfather taught me that anything worth doing was worth doing well.

(l. to r.) Barbara, Richard, Bill and Marge Crummett. Taken circa 1938 in Clinton, Maine.

My dad was a machine gunner in WWI. One of my uncles was in the cavalry and the other was in the artillery. In 1937, while visiting Waterville Airport, I talked my dad into paying for me to take a ride in a Piper Cub airplane…I loved it! By the time I graduated Lawrence High School in 1939, the Spanish Civil War had been fought and the war in Europe had started. Talking with my dad and uncles and doing lots of reading, I quickly decided that flying a plane in the Air Force was the way to fight. I didn't like what I had learned about the Army ground warfare and the Navy warfare on water.

Chapter 2

Choices and Anticipation

I wanted to join the Canadian Air Force when Britain declared war on Germany, but my dad wouldn't allow it. He felt that I was too young and in retrospect, he was right! I learned that to get into the U.S. Army Air Corps, one needed two years of college. I was accepted at Colby College and participated in Civilian Pilot Training. I took the Primary course in the spring semester, flying a J-3 Cub. The plane had a 50 or 60 horsepower engine, no brakes and a tail skid.

Once the instructor felt you were proficient, you could fly solo. We practiced short field take-offs and landings where there might be tall trees at the end or the beginning of the runway.

Tests by factory pilots had determined the maximum climb angle and the best airspeed at maximum power. It took concentration to achieve and maintain both specifications at once. With practice, you learned how much distance you had to have to get over a certain height of trees.

To make short-field landings in a Cub, you had to "slip" down at an angle, to make a landing as close to trees as you safely could. To make the plane "slip," you cut power and put your left wing down 40-50 degrees as you turned your plane's nose to the right 40-50 degrees.

This would slide you down sideways at a relatively steep angle of descent. Once past (below) trees, you had to quickly level wings, straighten plane's nose and you landed normally. You had to be conscious of the fact that you were flirting with a stall, and had to have enough speed when you rolled out of your slip, that you could have full control of the plane to make a nice landing.

In the fall semester, I took the Secondary course and flew a Waco UPF-7 biplane. They were open-cockpit, had 220 horsepower radial engines, a tail wheel and brakes. I flew solo in both planes within the normal time limit and found cross-country flights fun.

Generally had no trouble in spite of the fact that I got caught in a thunder storm in the Cub; with the Waco, I landed at a field with a foot of snow on the runway. I believe I was on the verge of hypothermia. It took about 45 minutes for me to get warm. Then, not knowing better, I went to the plane and managed to take off in that foot-deep snow and returned to the home field. I landed okay, but with the intense cold, probably around zero degrees, and me in normal winter clothes (no insulated flight suit), the cold draft coming back on me from the empty front cockpit for the 45 minute flight put me into hypothermia. It's a wonder I didn't crack up on landing! I had trouble getting out of the plane, I couldn't talk, it was difficult to walk and I couldn't stop shivering. It took at least an hour before I was warmed up.

After being checked out on take-offs and landings, stalls and spins, we began to do aerobatics; this was fun. However your body and brain are not used to multitudinous sensory signals and this often resulted in airsickness. Vomiting in an open cockpit plane is no fun. One day my plane's carburetor got iced up as I was doing snap rolls. Following standard operating procedure, I leaned the mixture of the engine until it backfired and blew the ice out – a unique experience! After winter came and the ice got thick on the Kennebec river (24-30"), above the dam at Shawmut near home, I landed on it. You can't tell when you've made contact; it's so smooth and silent. There's no screeching of tires and jolt, as the motionless tires have to start spinning at the speed of the plane.

One day I landed with a light coat of snow on the runway. I was on an icy path unknowingly and there must have been a slight crosswind, as my plane got slightly crabbed. Then I hit a bare spot. The plane began to ground loop, causing my left wing tip to brush the runway. I reacted instantly by hitting the throttle in order to blast air back, as I pushed full left rudder to stop it and got straightened out. Now, with full throttle, I aborted the landing and took off. I went around and came in for a second landing with no trouble. At least, not until I'd parked the plane and walked back to the terminal. There, I got a thorough chewing out by the instructors. They emphasized that if a wing is hit, the plane must be inspected before being flown again. (I don't recall that being mentioned during ground school, or by the Army Air Corps instructors).

After finishing the Primary CPT course, I applied for a pilot's license. I had to take a written and a flight test. I passed both and thus, I earned my private pilot's license. At last, I was a genuine flyboy! I stopped college at the end of my second-year spring semester in 1942, since I had my two years. In August, I enlisted in the Army Air Corps Reserve. We were in the war by then. My act of volunteering was a compulsory move on my part, since it insured I could fight in my chosen element. Plus, to wait to be drafted seemed to insult my patriotism and suggested a cowardly streak.

Chapter 3

Air Corps Initiation

I was called up and reported to the Portland recruiting station in February of 1943. With the initial written tests and screening to get into the Aviation Cadet Pilot Training unit, only 25% of our class made it! We got our uniforms and necessary inoculations at Ft. Devens, Mass. We spent a month in basic training at Nashville, Tenn. My memories of this time are of calisthenics, running the "Burma Road" obstacle course, guard duty, cold showers and K.P. March, 1943 saw me in preflight training at Maxwell Field, Alabama. I excelled scholastically. At the end of the month, they gathered a bunch of us into an accelerated group, and advanced us to the class of 43-I, nicknamed, "the whiz-kids," and shipped us out to Primary.

So April of '43 found me at Dorr Field in Arcadia, Florida in Primary flight training. Our plane was the Stearman PJ-17, a biplane somewhat similar to the Waco UPF-7 I'd flown, but there were big differences. The landing wheels were closer together, which made it more difficult handling on the ground and ground-looped very easily if you weren't paying attention. The ship had spoilers on the wings, too, so that it broke into a stall more quickly and violently. It was very rugged though and we learned to love it. It was fun doing aerobatics in it...a great trainer.

Aviation Cadet Richard M. Crummett.

Our instructor pilot was a big, 6'2", 220 lb. ex-policeman. I had no trouble; soloed in record time. Shortly, we were into aerobatics and having lots of fun. Our instructor figured it was time he humbled us "hot-rock" pilots, and took us up and did some new tricks we'd never seen—Cuban and Mexican "8's", outside loops and chandelles. And one other fancy maneuver that took us a couple days to figure out. What he did was start a snap-roll and then reverse it midway! We did a lot of low level flying, looking for alligators and flying in between trees to see how small an opening we could pass through.

They worked us hard; we were up at dawn and by lights-out at bedtime, we were all bushed. It was sort of like a country club. We had maids who cleaned our rooms, made our beds, and changed our linens. There was a laundry that did our uniforms and there was a tiled swimming pool with palm trees around it. Before we graduated in May of '43, they had us running around the (8-mile) field for calisthenics. When we first arrived, someone told us we would have to do this eventually and we thought they were just trying to scare us!

Chapter 4

Aviation Cadets

June '43 saw me at "Basic" flight school at Cochran field in Macon, Georgia, flying the BT-13 Vultee Vibrator. This was a great trainer in that it was difficult to make it perform well, doing precision aerobatics' maneuvers. It was easy on landings and take-off's though and we got our first taste of instrument and night-flying in this beast. It had a two-position prop and wing flaps. The fully enclosed canopy was a luxury compared to open cockpits. It had a 450 horsepower Pratt & Whitney engine and was much bigger and heavier than anything I'd flown.

On one of my cross-country flights it was hot in the cockpit, so I cracked the canopy open…the air felt good, but before I could react, the turbulent air sucked my map out through the opening. I had an English pilot for an instructor for a brief period. He was angry at being stuck over here teaching stupid American kids how to fly. He wanted to get into combat. He didn't like how I did my Immelmanns and he gave me a hard time. He had me fighting mad on more than one occasion, but I didn't lose my control or my temper. I began my night flying here. They had link-trainers to teach us the basics of instrument flight. Then we flew our planes with a hood over the cockpit to pass a test of our proficiency for basic instrument flight.

By August of '43, I was in Stuttgart, Arkansas at advanced flying school. We had AT-10 plywood Beechcraft twin-engine planes. We began to get into cross-country and instrument flying more seriously. Then, we started night cross-country trips. They put two students up on these night flights. The second pilot was supposed to sand-bag (go for a ride) in the right-hand seat, unless the pilot ran into trouble.

I had a hairy experience while sand-bagging for some unknown pilot (hope he was more on the ball in combat!). Our flight started normally and checkpoints came up fairly well, but not quite as expected. There were lots of little towns lit up at night down there. It wasn't long before I felt uneasy and started going over his flight plan and map. About then, our radio went out and we couldn't receive. Finally, I discovered an error in his course calculation. We were way off course in a sparsely settled area. With our radio receiver out, we couldn't pick up any navigational beams to locate ourselves. Gave him a rough course correction but then, our transmitter went out, too. We really felt lost by now. Before having to turn onto the final leg of our course, luck was with us. The moon was shining through the clouds and a particularly unique bend of the Mississippi glistened below. We had a fix!

May, 1943 graduating class of Aviation Cadets. (top row, l. to r.) Cauldwell, Giles, John, Pruden, Elliget, Crummett, Corley, Foster, Ogden, Heid. (middle row) Podesta, Elleswrath, Stott, MacIntosh, Hulquist, Coquillotte, Lang, Garman, Desso, Yeardley. (bottom row) Arnold, Weaver, Rosenberg, Nugarero, Robblin, Wray, Anderson, White.

Shortly thereafter, we ran smack dab over an airfield with planes up night flying. Boy, we had lights flashing by us everywhere. Probably they got just as big a scare as we did. Anyhow, we set a course for home, figured our time of arrival and damn! The gas began to look like we might have a problem making it. By the time the gas gauge was getting low and approaching empty, we still couldn't see our home field's flashing beacon. Always wanted to parachute but looking out into the blackness and thinking of jumping wasn't fun. Finally we saw the beacon and landed okay but in taxiing back to park, one engine quit. This was probably good training for the stressful and strange experiences we would have in combat. Anyhow, I was mighty pleased and proud to graduate and get my 2nd Lieutenants commission. After a brief leave to go home, I was ordered to report to the 397th bomb group at Tampa, Florida, McDill Field.

Chapter 5

Introduction to the Marauder: Love at First Sight

Reporting to the 397th, I was assigned to the 598th Squadron as a co-pilot. We were in the latter part of our transition training, for the B-26 Marauder Medium Bomber, built by Martin. I fell in love with this plane during my first flight in it; it was so powerful, fast and robust, it seemed to be indestructible. It had flush rivets so its outer surfaces were smooth. Those two big 13-foot four-bladed propellers and the 2000 horsepower Pratt & Whitney engines were awesome. We flew with different pilots as we trained.

My dad and I at the farm. Taken September, 1943.

We new pilots didn't know the Martin B-26 had acquired a bad reputation. It was known as "the widow maker" and the people of Tampa, Florida said of our plane, "One a day in Tampa Bay." The wartime urgency to produce advanced model planes resulted in Martin's amazing performance of starting with blueprints in September of 1939 winning a 200 plane contract. They built a new plant, hired and trained workers (mostly women) and started production while the plant construction was still in progress. His first plane rolled out November of 1940. There were no test or "proof" models. As soon as the prop's were installed and the plane was complete, the Air Force was notified; they sent pilots over and flew them away.

The old experienced Air Force pilots and mechanics took them "as is" with all the bugs and gremlins associated with any new product. They managed to use them without any accidents. Once the new pilots graduated and the new mechanics got into them, we had lots of problems and crashes. It took a while for proper procedures to be established, new methods and techniques laid down from the old experienced people, to clear our beautiful "big hairy bird's" reputation. General Jimmy Doolittle helped!

Our group's pilots had completed most of their transition training in the B-26. They'd spent several months already at different bases learning combat techniques. Higher command reasoned that they could put twice as many planes overseas, if they put the fully trained pilot in the left seat and a green pilot (that's us!) in the right seat as co-pilot. So, inasmuch as I had signed up to be a pilot, I was then stuck with being a co-pilot. I was disappointed but I accepted my fate stoically. I prayed that somehow soon, I'd get my 1st pilot rating in the B-26 and be in the left seat with my own plane and crew.

On 14October1943, we moved to Avon Park bombing range for more training. I soon had my first flight in the Martin B-26, nicknamed, "the Baltimore Whore," due to her short wingspan and no visible means of support! Maybe that is why I was seduced so quickly. What a thrill on that first take-off, feeling the tremendous acceleration as you sped racing down the runway. I loved it. What a ship. Wow!

We co-pilots got cram courses on the plane and all its mechanical operating components, electrical and hydraulic systems, so we could perform our co-pilot duties. Our duties were:

A preflight inspection of the plane, checking condition of tires, landing gear, engines, propellers, control surfaces, wings and particularly looking for fluid leaks. In the plane, we went through the checklist as we got the two engines started, taxied out and took off. At the pilots direction we raised and lowered the landing gear, set and raised flaps, set the rpm of the engine and propellers, adjusted cowl flaps to control oil and engine temperature and checked all gauges indicating pressure, temperature and quantities of fuel, etc. The only controls we didn't touch (unless the pilot told us to) were the flight controls, throttles and the engine switches.

In emergencies, we had to lower the landing gear via a secondary system, or transfer fuel from one tank to another, should one engine fail (she would fly safely on one!). We also monitored all flight control instruments, especially during instrument or night flying, to make sure the pilot wasn't making any mistakes due to vertigo or anoxia. Should we sense trouble, we'd alert him and if he could snap out of it (most did), fine.

We continued combat practice. Dropped many practice bombs at the bombing range, developing the close-knit coordination between the bombardier and pilot which is necessary to score good accuracy. Shot for practice at tow-targets and dye spots, which we threw into the ocean. Scoring hits required learning to judge relative motion. This was more difficult than trap or skeet shooting. Anyone who learned wing shooting from bird hunting, adapted his leads quickly and easily.

Chapter 6

Getting to the Fight

Then, 1November1943, we moved to Hunter Field at Savanna, Georgia, where we got new B-26C planes and we were issued 45 Colt semi-automatic pistols with a shoulder holster. We got other supplies and equipment in preparation for going overseas. Lt. Donald Stangle chose me to be his co-pilot; I would fly with him from then until I'd flown 55 missions, with a few exceptions, which I will try to record here.

From here we flew submarine patrols out over the Atlantic. Formation flying began to include forming up into multi-plane formations. Soon, we had flights of four or more forming up into a squadron of three flights. We then went on maneuvers and practiced simulated combat operations. Finally, after New Year's '44, we were judged ready. Our ground forces packed up and shipped out for overseas.

In the latter part of February, 1944, the main group of the 397th left Hunter Field to fly over to Europe via South America and then Africa and north. Two planes piloted by Lieutenants Stangle and Patterson were left behind to follow later. All the ground personnel would go to England by boat. Boy, was I glad I was flying over. I'd learned the Nazi U-boats had been sinking some of our ships! When we got back together in England, those who went by boat told us it was no picnic. It was a pretty rough trip and rather longer than they expected.

Finally on 25February1943, we left Hunter Field and went to Miami, Florida, where we landed and picked up a celestial navigator to guide us. Flight duration was 2:35. Our crews only consisted of pilot, co-pilot and engineer. After the navigator came on 28thFebruary, we left and went to Puerto Rico. Flight time 4:55. Beautiful overwater flight; nice airfield; great Officer's Club. Purchased a few goodies (booze, silk stockings, perfumed soaps).

On the 29thFebruary, we flew to Trinidad. Flight time 3:55. Pretty little islands were seen below in a nice blue ocean. Looked wild and primitive down there and was beginning to get hot and humid. Reckoned we were getting down into the tropics. Enroute we overtook a B-24 and had some fun; we couldn't resist acquainting them with our B-26 marauder. So, we dove under them and came up in front of them—putting them in our prop wash. Boy, did we wake them up! They really bounced around.

On 1March, we flew to Belem, Brazil over a continuous dense frightful jungle. Duration of flight was 6:40. It was hot, humid and the runway on the field was black-top of some kind. The surface was sticky and the heels of your shoes would sink in 1/2 inch if you stood still; it rained three or four times, with the sun blazing down in between showers. On 2March, we left early in the morning when it was supposed to be cooler. Stangle and I had to use the full length of the runway and then struggled to get over the trees off a little bit, sweating it out with our hearts pounding as we barely cleared them. Finally, off into the blue, we headed for Natale, Brazil. Flight time was 5:20. Lt. Patterson, following us, didn't make it; he couldn't get off and up, crashing in the jungle, but everyone survived. They hitched a ride over on a B-24 following us.

We found the Natale Field a good place. Temperatures were more normal with less humidity, and we were able to finally get our laundry done. Did some shopping at their nice BX and bought a pair of nice cowhide boots, while our engineer checked out the plane. As at Belem, Natale personnel warned us not to try to date any of the local girls. Most of them were infected with V.D. Anyhow, had an extra day's rest before attempting to cross the Atlantic.

On 4 March, we left for Ascension Island, out in the middle of the Atlantic Ocean. Duration of flight was 7:35. When our ETA came up, we couldn't see an island! Our navigator had no explanation at to whether we were north or south of our destination. We didn't have gas enough to return to Brazil or go to Africa. We had a real crisis since we were not allowed to use our radio; we had a life raft in the plane and the '26 was supposed to stay up for 13 seconds if you ditched it into the water. I am a cool-headed sort, so I started studying the area around us. Off to our right, south, I saw a cloud, small and far away; I hadn't seen one all day as we flew. I got Stangle's attention, pointed out the cloud and told him that I believed that under that cloud was our island. He said, "I think you may be right." We turned, went south and sure enough, there was that beautiful little island! The runway started at the ocean on one end and went to the ocean at the other end, with a rise in the middle. Wide-Awake Field was cut into the side of a volcano.

On 5 March, we left for Roberts Field in Liberia, Africa. Flight time was 5:20. We had no trouble and landed okay. It was a wild, jungle sort of place with natives wandering around. Our barracks were built on posts about five feet tall, so they were open underneath. We were told that the natives might sneak in to steal things during the night. I slept with my 45 under my pillow and took my valuables into bed with me, tucking in the sides of the mosquito netting under me. I thought I heard something moving around underneath, before I fell asleep, but didn't hear anything afterwards. They did come in and went through our bags—I didn't seem to be missing any property, but my things weren't arranged the way I'd left them!

6 March, we left for a field at Dakar, French West Africa. Flight time was 4:00. This place was more civilized, but we saw our first sight of war. There were some destroyed trucks and an old rusty burned-out tank nearby. On 7 March, we flew over the western part of the Sahara Desert, which seemed to be mostly rocky, with no trees or vegetation, until we crossed a mountain range (Atlas?); on the north side, it was all green with grass and trees right up to Marrakech, Morocco. Duration of flight was 6:30. This was a French field, very neat and clean. They treated us as princes. Putting us up in a wonderful white resort hotel-like building and feeding us like we were kings.

We were warned not to go into the city nearby, especially the old section, the Medina, where the native Arabs lived. You could buy all kinds of souvenirs and find exotic entertainments. Seems like some previous outfit had an adventurous smart-ass who just couldn't stay on base. At night, he snuck into the city. He never came back. They sent M.P.'s in looking for him. They saw a man wearing his shoes and other people who had on different pieces of his clothing, but no trace of him!

Our longest over-water flights so far were the two 7:35 and 5:20 segments crossing the Atlantic. I was getting sick of flying over water in our Marauder. Our normal range of the B-26 is about five hours. They had put an extra gas tank in our bomb bay to extend our range. Our next segment of our trip would be much longer than any so far, and would all be over water; I didn't know our maximum range and looked ahead with trepidation.

8March, we left for England. To get there we had to fly west into the Atlantic, turn and go north so we would be beyond the intercept armed patrols the Nazi's flew to shoot us down from France. We couldn't fly over Spain or Portugal, as apparently they would notify the enemy. Finally, when we got up west of England, we'd turn east and hopefully, if our navigation was good, we'd come into it okay. We finally saw land and landed at St. Mawgan, Newquay, on the southwest corner of Great Britain in Wales, after 8:40 hours over the ocean. I could've got out and kissed the terra firma! Some fellow greeted us as we disembarked, but I couldn't understand a word he said. (I didn't know the people there had their own dialect and didn't speak English unless it was necessary). However, I knew it wasn't French or German, so I relaxed.

Chapter 7

Preparation for Combat

We stayed there until 11 March, when we took off and joined our 397th group at Gosfield Field, Braintree, Essex. Flight time was 3:25. We learned we'd have to retrain, as new tactics were required to survive and be successful, bombing enemy installations. Our stateside training was all wrong for the new techniques and advanced technologies of the enemy!

This was to be our home for a while. We lived in metal Quonset huts. We had little sheet-metal stoves, but no fuel—were these buildings cold—snow was on the ground. We slept on cots and had three heavy wool blankets folded up under me and four on top, and you were still cold! Don Stangle and I got a crosscut saw and started making firewood. I found an axe and split some logs and soon we had a nice fire in our stove; we were envied. We loaned our tools to others (city slickers) who quickly learned it wasn't as easy as it looked. We had a few chuckles watching them curse and struggle.

There were trenches outside, alongside our barracks, which we were told we should use, if the air raid siren sounded. The first night when the siren went off, we jumped out of bed, slipped on our sheepskin flight boots and a jacket, ran out and jumped into the trench. Wow. Seems like some fellows had been urinating in the trench, instead of walking over to the latrine. After that, when we heard the siren, we just rolled over and went back to sleep—unless there seemed to be a show going on above worth watching.

We were all issued G.I. bicycles like the European military used. They were big and heavy, but very rugged. Rode around the base and even rode into Braintree nearby. I had a perplexing time becoming familiar with English money and how to read the prices of goods. First thing, I bought was a hot loaf of bread; my nose lead me via the wonderful aroma to a bakery. Boy, was it good! We split it up and ate it on the spot. We spent a week getting settled in and then began to fly again.

Here, at night, the Nazi bombers came over targeting industrial areas near by. We learned what ground anti-aircraft artillery (AAA guns) could do, as we saw the British shoot down some of them…many flaming as they fell. The Brits at times threw up a box barrage, creating a cube-like space filled with exploding shells. God was this horrible. It was deadly: most effective. We hoped the Nazi's didn't have this knowledge (they did!).

I began to get more instruction on flying our B-26 Marauder. They told us our planes would probably work great if we'd drop our bombs from 10,000 feet. Inasmuch as the Nazi 88mm AAA guns are very accurate at that altitude, we'd developed an evasive action technique which should minimize our losses. In addition, the French resistance had identified most of the areas that were heavily defended. Normally, we'd detour around these unless the location was a target.

We were assigned to the Ninth Tactical Air Force. It was mainly medium B-26 bombers, whereas the Eighth was mainly heavy bombers. Our job would be to hit tactical targets that our ground forces were having difficulty defeating, as well as concentrations of Nazi men, materials and supplies. As we began to destroy their transportation infrastructure, we hit bridges, tunnels, railroad yards, submarine pens, ports and airfields. Soon, we were known as "the bridge busters."

(l. to r.) Lt. Norman Scherer, our Navigator; Captain Don Stangle, my pilot and Lt. Dick Crummett, Co-pilot. Taken at Gosfield, England.

My pilot Lt. Stangle, had me practice landings and takeoffs on several occasions until I became proficient doing them. It was fun, because I had developed an understanding of the plane's limitations and capabilities. I became comfortable handling her. A lot of my knowledge came from observing my pilot perform the different maneuvers in forming up in "flights" of six ships. Then, the flights formed into an 18-ship V-shaped "box." When we flew a mission, we'd have two boxes in echelon formation. We practiced until everyone knew how to take-off at 20-second intervals and form flights, boxes and the 36-ship "mission" group.

Chapter 8

Engaging the Enemy

Finally, they loaded bombs in our planes and we took off with a full 6-man crew. All guns armed with ammo, we flew a practice diversionary mission. We went to Berk-Sur-Mere, France on the coast, but turned away about five miles from target and returned home. Soon, on 15April, 1944, we moved to Rivenhall Field and the Ninth Air Command declared we were combat-ready. Now we were able to join the other eight Ninth Air Force B-26 groups here in the fight!

There were other groups of B-26 Marauders. The British, Free-French, Australians, and South Africans also had Marauder squadrons. We knocked down bridges from Belgium to Southern France. At the beginning, bombs were in short supply. If we couldn't drop, due to our target being obscured by clouds, for instance, we brought the bombs home. Later, when bombs were more plentiful, we could drop them on auxiliary targets or dump them in the Channel.

The following mission information (from my diary, and with memory permitting) is organized by:

Date, Plane number, Pilot, Position in *formation, Bomb-load, Flight duration, Target, Location, Amount of flak, and Comments.

*Formation was as illustrated below:

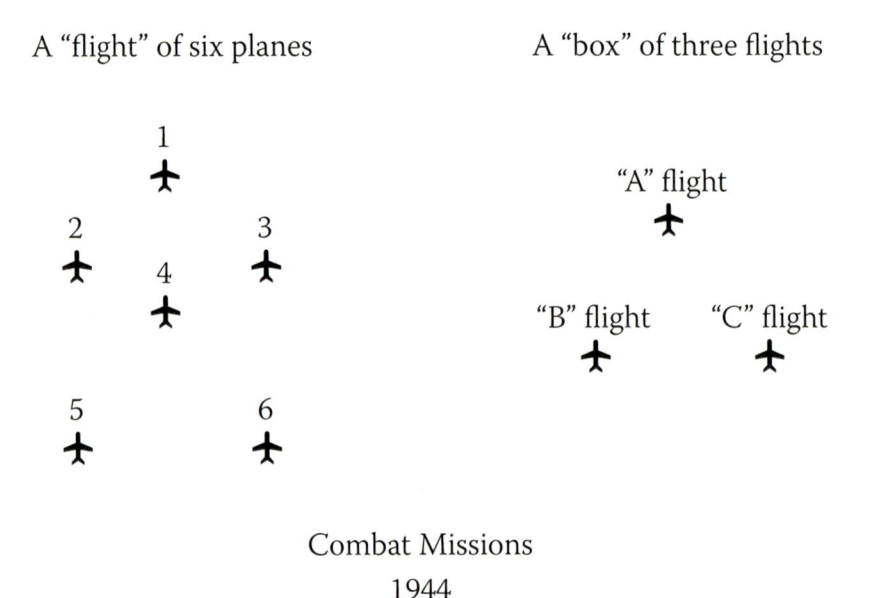

A "flight" of six planes   A "box" of three flights

```
        1
        ✈

    2       3                    "A" flight
    ✈   4   ✈                        ✈
        ✈
                            "B" flight    "C" flight
    5       6                   ✈             ✈
    ✈       ✈
```

Combat Missions
1944

19April, 161, 4X1000, 2:30, first mission to Berk sur Mer, France. Boy, we were very apprehensive (scared!). The mission was a "milk run"; no AAA flak and no fighters came up to greet us. It was a nice clear sunny day and it looked so neat and peaceful there. Hey, maybe this isn't going to be so bad after all.

20April, 161, 8X500, 2:55, "No-ball" (V-1 rocket site) at Le Plouey Ferme. Good hits on target. We experienced no opposition, neither flak nor fighters. We did a lot of sweating on this one since we expected the worst. All the fear and tension we had helped us to realize that anticipating was our enemy. We had to stop anticipating. Believe that at this time, I began to make the necessary philosophical mental rearrangement and adjustment one must have to survive in a war. Killing and being killed must become accepted as routine daily occurrences in the course of performing one's duty, and not be traumatic experiences.

A moment of prayer before our mission. (l. to r.) Sgt. Snow, turret gunner; Capt. Stangle, Pilot; Sgt. Adams, tail-gunner; Lt. Crummett, co-pilot. Taken at Rivenhall Field, England.

21 April, 161, 8X500, 2:30, No-ball at Bois de Coupelle, light flak, AAA shell bursts were black puffs—ugly. Dropped okay on the first run. Germans shot anti-aircraft artillery guns at us. This was the first time we saw flak. The sound was a "woomph" kind of like if you were in a metal can and a firecracker burst outside.

25 April, 161, 8X500, 3:10, No-ball at Bois de Cocquerel. Made bomb run but couldn't drop due to smoke, haze and clouds obscuring target.

26 April, 161, 4X1000, 2:25, Railroad yards at St. Grislain. Didn't drop due to weather.

27 April, 161, I A 3, 4X1000, 3:05, Gun batteries at Ouistreham, excellent hits on target.

30 April, 161, I C 7, 4X1000, 2:05, No-ball site at Lottingham, moderate accurate flak. Some of the planes got several holes. Shrapnel from the shells hitting your plane sounds like someone throwing rocks at your car.

1 May, 161, 4X1000, 3:30, Railroad bridge at Montes Grasstcourt, bulls-eye on target.

2 May, 161, II B 1, 8X500 "b", 3:30, Railroad marshalling yards at Businessgny, France.

8 May, 161, I C 4, 4X1000, 3:35, Railroad bridge at Dissel, France (near Rouen), intense accurate flak. Wow. Horrifying. Believe a few of our planes were shot down. Learned that some of those German gunners can really shoot.

10 May, 161, I C 1, 4X1000, 3:20, Railroad storage and repair sheds at Creil, France, good hits.

11 May, 160, Pilot McEachern, I C 3, 16X250, 3:00, Airfield at Beaumont Le Roger. I flew back as Pilot. McEachern threw up his hands after leaving the target area and shouted over to me, "I've had it" and stopped flying the plane. I had to take over the controls! Really worked my butt off because I flew formation too close to

lead ship—vortex from his wing had me fighting to hold a steady position; a learning experience.

12May, 161, II D 1, 4X1000, Railroad guns battery at Etaples, bulls-eye on target with moderate accurate flak.

19May, 161, Pilot Bronson, I A 1, 4X1000, Coastal defense guns at St. Ciely. Hit bulls-eye; intense accurate flak. We caught them by surprise and they tried to ruin our day, too.

22May, 163, Pilot McEachern, I A 7, 4X1000, St. Marie au Bosc, dropped bombs by pathfinder. I flew one hour formation. Tucked-in too tight! But I did much better this time.

24May, 161 II A 4, 4X1000, 2:10, Harbor installations at Dieppe, France, bulls-eye with intense accurate flak. Wow. Most heavily defended target we had run into so far. They sure didn't want us to get that one. We had our baptism by fire—it can't get worse than this. Wasn't scared. Too damn busy doing my job for that. You just concentrate on your duties and completely ignore the bursting shells.

25May, 161, II A 4, 2X2000, 3:15, Railroad bridge at Liege, Belgium, intense accurate flak at target. Going back home, eight FW190 fighters passed us and did not fire at us. They were probably out of ammo and going home too. What a birthday gift! I am 22.

26May, 161, 2X2000, 3:25, Airfield repair depot at Chartres, good hits, light accurate flak.

27May, 161, 2X2000, Railroad bridge at Le Manoir (S.E. of Rouen), light accurate flak.

31May, 161, II B 1, 2X2000, 3:20, Highway bridge at Rouen, intense flak. Damn! We missed; navigator inadvertently hit the PDI switch while moving around in the nose and the bombardier and pilot didn't realize it until it was too late. This switch was the Pilot Direction Indicator; enables the bombardier to tell the pilot to move the plane to the left or right so he can get the bombsight crosshairs onto the target arming point.

2June, 132, I A 4, 2X2000, 1:55, Coastal gun batteries at Camiers, excellent hits on target. I got some formation flying "stick"-time and did pretty well.

3June, 129, II A 4, 2X2000, 2:45, Coastal gun batteries at Le Havre, good hits, intense accurate flak. This was a rough one; on returning we noticed our plane was full of holes.

Following some missions, when we got accurate flak, we had quite a few planes make it back home, but then crack up upon landing. I saw many of these crack-ups and crashes. Sometimes, some of the crew got out of the crashed plane, and sometimes it caught fire. Occasionally the fellows couldn't or were unable to get out of the plane and they burned, while the ammo for the machine guns began popping off. A few planes had bombs on board and after a while, they would explode.

Lt. Coyne, our bombardier, up in the nose at the Norden bombsight. When heavy flak came up, what a view he had!

I believe what caused the crashes was that the shrapnel had damaged the landing gear or one of the main gear's tires. On touching down, many went down on one side—the wing and prop hitting the ground, causing the plane to swerve off the runway. Anything could happen then. One planes engine mount broke, and the engine, with the prop still spinning, flew up and over onto the fuselage, chopping a big hole just behind the cockpit. Broken gas, oil and hydraulic fluid lines ignited in the nacelle and set the wing on fire—which destroyed the ship.

Some planes elected to keep their gear up and landed on their belly. Those that landed on the grass beside the runway, shutting off their engines before hitting the ground, generally survived the best.

5June, 161, Leader of "window element" for a pathfinder mission, group-bombing through clouds with some instrument flying.

Chapter 9

Busting Bridges

6 June (D-Day), 161, 20X100, 5:00, Gun batteries in Trouville. We awoke that morning and much to our surprise, our planes had been painted overnight with five, one-foot wide stripes…alternating black and white. These "invasion stripes" were worn on all our planes so our troops could identify us as "friendly." We soon learned we'd put up a mission of 36 planes, who'd been due over the landing beaches prior to 7:00 AM. Wow!

They'd have taken off in stormy rain, with low clouds and also in the dark, about 5:00AM. These poor devils must have been awakened around 2:30 AM. I flew after lunch, when planes returning were quickly gassed up and reloaded with bombs. We'd been briefed: our targets were the gun emplacements behind the beach. I saw ships and boats by the hundreds. Several big battleships were lined up off shore, firing broadside (all nine cannons at once!). It was an awesome sight. Our boys had landed!

Along the shore the boats were a haphazard mess; you could see that many had been badly shot-up and sunk or damaged. There was a lot of smoke near the beach. The sky was full of our bombers, coming and going. No Nazi fighter planes or AAA fire was noticed. Of course, with all the air traffic that day, we all had to exit target area at once, on a Westerly course, to clear the beach combat area, and then, safely out in the English Channel, turn North to return to England.

B-26 Marauder, with "invasion" stripes.

7June, 138, Railroad yards. Big fight going on down below!
8June, 161, 16X250, Railroad loading ramp at Flers, bulls-eye.
13June, 161, 8X500, Oil dump at Foret D'Andaine, bulls-eye, lots of fire and secondary explosions.

14June, 161, 2X2000, 3:30, Railroad bridge near Chartres, France, got direct hits, moderate but very accurate flak. Wow!

18June, 140, 8X500, 2:45, No-ball site at Bachmont, "pathfinder" through clouds, light accurate flak. Pathfinder was a technology developed by the Brit's using radio beams as a guidance tool. When the beams intersected, we were on target.

Sgt. Robert Adams, our engineer/tail gunner, in London. The ruined building in the background was the sad result of a Nazi "buzz" bomb, or V-1 rocket.

22June, 161, II C 1, 4X1000, Fortified positions at Nourinville, near Cherbourg. Very accurate flak; our navigator got a shrapnel wound in his hand that nearly tore his thumb off. I bandaged his hand and later was complimented on this by the flight surgeon. Our number 4 plane was shot down on this mission. We had a close call! The flight leaders (us!) are always the prime target for fighters or AAA gunners.

24June, 129, 2X2000, 4:05, Railroad bridge at Maison la Fitte, west of Paris. This target was heavily defended. They threw up a box barrage at our release point. Four planes were shot down over area (161 was one of them). Everyone was full of holes. We had over 100 in our plane.

The time between combat missions was precious. One had to do something to busy his mind with things other than the war. In England, we had an officers' club for us to socialize in. There was usually a bar where one could get drinks, and different set-ups of tables and chairs for informal meetings, reading and games; poker and chess. Not liking cards, I got into playing chess. This was wonderful because it required deep concentration and a game could last several hours—time just flew by so fast. I remember that an English pastor came in and played about 10 of us; he'd spend only about 15 seconds with each of us to make his moves, and he beat all of us.

For me, downtime on base was more or less a solitary affair. I'd read old letters and write letters to the folks back home. The more missions I flew, the more I isolated myself from socializing with the men in our barracks. I reckon it was an involuntary emotional defensive act.

30June, 139, 3:55, Highway intersection at Thury Harcourt, France. Didn't drop. Dumped bombs in Channel on the way home.

6July, 141, 8X500, 4:00, Railroad bridge at St. Germain. Saw Nazi tanks on the roads below. Panzer unit?

8July, 136, 4:00, Pilot was Group C. O., Col. Coiner, leading window element at Samur, France. Got rime ice on ship. Horrible weather!

Chapter 10

Rest and Relaxation

To keep up morale, a reward system was set up. Every five missions, you were awarded the air medal (technically, I earned 18 of these!). Every 25 missions you were given five days or a week's leave for rest and recreation. Depending on your circumstance and location, you had no problem getting off base at night to go to nearby cities and towns. In England, I sometimes hopped on my bike and pedaled into town for a pint and some darts on most nights. As long as you made it back the next morning ready to fly, nobody complained.

With my new acquaintance, an English nurse, along, it was much easier to get to know the local people. We were invited to tea many times. I thought the English seemed pretty much like out folks back home. Once you got to be friends with them, they would do anything for you.

My nurse and I biked around trying to find a stream to go swimming. We found some pretty ones, but on those days, it was so cold that the thought of skinny dipping didn't seem so attractive. I saw some nice English farms. They had lots of crop damage from the large burrowing hares. These pesky things seemed to live in colonies in the woods and would dig up quite a large area. We saw lots of fat ring-necked pheasants too. Was tempted to shoot one for the pot but all game belonged to the "Crown," so I knew better.

On one of my 48-hour passes, I learned quickly that in London particularly, English and American are rather different languages—what a shocker. I had a lot of fun riding around on the upper deck of their double- decker buses. Riding in their old taxi cabs was a unique experience too. They sure were built well to have survived so long.

Exploring the subway was not too bad; the local folks were helpful if you got lost. I did (naively) accept help from some older gentleman who assisted me in finding a place to stay. He said it was much closer and cheaper than the place recommended for us Americans to billet. He was most kind. He made sure the lady who rented me the room had given me enough blankets and even showed me how to light the gas fireplace in the room. It was only when he kept hanging around and he offered to "tuck me in" that I suddenly realized something wasn't right. I thanked him again and told him he would have to leave—now!

I got to meet an upper class English girl and visited the theatre—very nice. Through her I got into one of the private social clubs. Boy. That was a very fancy old establishment; met some typical old English gentleman, very well to do. I applied for membership and surprisingly got accepted. I received my membership card months later. I never did get back to visit the club.

Above the Clouds

9July to 16July: My first 25-mission R&R leave, I had a horseback ride that nearly got me killed!

From our base at Rivenhall, I took a trip to some castle which had been converted into a reception center...it was like a resort hotel. I was dumbfounded the first morning when an elderly English butler-type person awakened me and inquired what kind of juice or fruit did I prefer. Then, I learned that he would serve it to me in bed! This happened every morning. Breakfast, lunch and dinner were home-cooked by an excellent kitchen staff. As I recall, we even had a menu to choose from. Then, between meals, they put out treats to snack on with punch or fruit juice to drink. All this —in the midst of severe rationing to the general public. It was like being in heaven.

There was a list of daily activities posted on a bulletin board. You could engage in sports, take sightseeing tours or just browse around the estate and grounds. I can remember doing some skeet shooting one day; they had nice ranges set up and I had it all to myself. Shot to my heart's content. I tried archery with a couple of guys but had trouble mastering the English long bow...I couldn't hit a thing.

I elected to ride horseback one day. Found my horse a fidgety thing with an English saddle. Holy Cow. I'd only ridden a pony before, except for riding our draft horses bareback as a kid. The stirrups were way up, so you couldn't get a grip on the horse with your legs. Boy. Wondered if I could stay on and not fall off! With trepidation, I mounted up.

Half the ride was spent leading some horses out to pasture. For some reason my horse just didn't seem to want to walk like all the other horses. He kept prancing and wanted to trot. I had to rein him in hard to prevent this, but he'd keep trying. This had me pulling on the reins with one hand and tugging on the halter rope of the horse I was leading with the other. Reckon we went two miles to reach the pasture where we dropped off the horses we'd lead out. My arms were tired by then, as well as my back and butt from all that rough jouncing.

On the ride back, my horse still wanted to trot. Finally, I thought maybe he just wanted to get ahead of the others and perhaps if I let him trot a little he would settle down. Anyhow, my arms were tired from tugging on the reins. So I relaxed on the reins a bit and he immediately broke into a gallop! I hadn't counted on this. I tried to slow him down by pulling on the reins, but I guess he had the bit in his teeth, because I couldn't stop him. I wound up grabbing a handful of mane and hung on for dear life.

He galloped down this road into a small village where the road had a 30-degree turn. I prayed I wouldn't fall off; what I didn't know was that he was smooth-shod. When we hit the turn, he slipped and nearly went down, and I nearly fell off. It was a wonder that we didn't hit parked cars along the curb. There was no slowing him down now. Next, we came to a major highway with barricades up on either side. My guts tightened. Well, by then we'd reached the barrier and the horse jumped and we soared over it, landing right on the edge of a four-lane divided expressway. Car tires screeched, horns blared, and my some miracle, I managed to stay on his back. The horse made it unscathed across the highway and sailed over the second barricade okay.

The rest of the ride wasn't so bad; by now I'd learned how to balance myself pretty well. He galloped all the way back to the stable. I kicked my feet clear of the stirrups and gratefully slid off his back. He was lathered up from his run. Next, the owner appeared and started to give me hell. She blamed me for running the horse too hard! She said I'd made him lame; by golly, he might've pulled a muscle when he slipped. I did my best to explain what happened and apologized profusely for my lack of horsemanship in controlling him. She didn't believe a word of my explanation and she began to question my status as a gentleman, which made me mad (but I bit my tongue and stayed silent).

On our last day, they invited some nurses over from the English and American staffed hospitals nearby for a party. We had punch, cake and ice cream and there was music and dancing. The nurses were pretty and nice, but naturally, the party didn't last long enough!

Chapter 11

Hammering the Nazis

18 July, 119, 16X260, 3:55, Fragmentation bombs loaded with RDX, Enemy troop concentration at Caen, France, moderate but accurate flak. Two planes had to make belly landings and three lost control as they landed and cracked up when they got back to home base. One caught on fire.

19July, 119, 4X1000, Railroad bridge at Sheriay, France, moderate, accurate flak.

21July, 141, 2:30, Got checked out as first pilot, limited to daytime flights only. (Still stuck in the co-pilot's seat, with Don Stangle as pilot).

25July, 119, 16X260, 3:00, Fragmentation RDX, Large concentration of Nazi infantry, equipment and supplies at Montreuil, France, southwest of St. Lo. Each flight bombed a rectangular area adjoining another flight's, so we covered a large portion, with other

9th Air Force groups bombing adjacent sections. We blasted a hole in the Nazi line for Patton's tanks and infantry to dash through.

26July, 119, 4X1000, Railroad bridge.

28July, 119, 4X1000, Railroad bridge at Courcelles, France, pathfinder, bombing through clouds by boxes, light flak. Got to fly some formation stick-time.

31July, 119, 4X1000, 3:15, Railroad bridge in Mayenne, France. Pathfinder box-bombing through clouds.

2August, 119, 2X2000, 4:35, Railroad bridge near Tours, France. Returned almost out of gas!

5August, Moved to Hurn Field, Bornemouth, Great Britain. This move brought us closer to the enemy. The group celebrated the completion of 100 combat missions here. I believe I had completed about 40 by then.

This was a nice, clean and comfortable base. The barracks and officer's club was located in a hilly area. Living here was good—can't recall anything to gripe about. The city was close and bus transportation was convenient. I spent some time in the city window-shopping, sightseeing, and found the people polite and friendly. Ventured only once or twice down to the beach areas. Marveled at the girls changing into their swimsuits and back again with only a towel to conceal themselves. Don't remember going swimming. Guess the water was pretty cold.

We all had a big celebration at the club on our group's 100th mission. We put out invitations to get as many girls to come as possible. Boy. Response was outstanding. We wound up with about one gal for every guy. They were in a mood to let their hair down and so everyone danced, drank and partied till they couldn't stand anymore!

Think this was where I got the most tasty fish & chips, in a cone made from newspaper. An English nurse I knew came from this area. She showed me around the city on foot and by bike; it was a vacation spot for the English and an enjoyable place if you knew where to go.

7August, 119, 8X500, 3:45, Railroad bridge at Neuvy sur Loire, light accurate flak. Lots of fighting on the ground in this area.

10August, 136, 2X2000, 4:15, Railroad bridge at Nogent sur Seine, hit bullseye. Our right wingman, Capt. Cooper, got hit on the first flak barrage from enemy gunners below, while we were on the bombing run. His ship moved away, on fire. A man on fire exited the plane sitting on top of one of the salvoed bombs as they dropped. Cooper was later picked up by the French resistance and moved from safe house to safe house, up and over the Pyrennes and made it back to England!

11August, 118, 2X2000, Railroad bridge at Oissel, near Rouen, intense accurate flak, shot up badly, full of holes. Our tough hairy bird brought us all home though.

13August, 119, I A 1, 16X250, Highway area near Broglie, France. Don Stangle flew a swell, smooth lead. Great job!

14August, 128, 16X250, Highway bridge and road junction near St. Martin de la Lieue.

15August, 124, 28X100 oil-rubber bombs, 2:45, St. Malo citadel fortification. The 394th Bomb Group hit this target before us with 1000-pounder's to make some kindling for us so we could get a good fire going!

16August, 128, 4X1000, Railroad bridge at Neuvy, northeast of Caen, Pathfinder mission, dropped bombs by box through clouds.

17August, 158, I A 1, Pilot was 598th Squadron C.O., Maj. Allen, 4X1000 at Brion, France, Pathfinder mission. Rough one. We hit right wing tip parking the plane.

20August, 158, 16X260 fragmentation "B", Area target was enemy troop concentration at Foret de la Londe, moderate flak.

Major Richard M. Crummett

26August, 4118, 16X260 fragmentation, 2:45Waterfront target at Rouen, France, intense accurate flak. This was a rough one!

Chapter 12

A-26 Field, Dreux: Onward into France

1 September, moved from Hurn Field, Bournemouth, U.K. to A-26 Field at Gonfreville, Normandy, France.

Our Field, A-26, was a pierced steel planking strip on packed dirt. It was alright till it rained…water made soft spots appear and the PSP bent under the 40, 000-pound weight of our planes. The bent edges where the strip sections joined exposed sharp, protruding edges which cut the tires of our planes badly, causing many to be replaced.

We were out in the country living in large pyramid-type tents. I had two other guys in with me and we slept on cots. A slit or straddle-trench was our latrine. You had to bring a shovel to cover your defecation. We ate standing up, but had a rough board-counter to rest your mess kit on. This mess area was under a big, long wall tent. The food wasn't like our bases in England, but at least it was hot. We had competition with yellow-jacket hornets though, especially when you got anything sweet. You ate carefully, lest one get in your mouth; got stung on my knuckle one day and it swelled up to twice its normal size.

We washed our mess kits by first scraping all garbage into large cans; then, you dunked your mess kit into a big can of boiling soapy water an finally into clear boiling water for a rinse. Water was provided in two-wheeled tank trailer units. You were only to draw out a canteen full at a time. To shave, you hung your mirror on a tent pole and poured some water into your steel helmet. We didn't get to bathe all the time we were there. Luckily, I bought some extra underwear and socks before we left England.

In our free time, those adventurous types among us…me and my two tent mates, would take walks on the roads around our camp. I found a box of American pineapple grenades lying in a ditch one day and we decided to try them out. We had our own little fourth of July. When they exploded, though, the wicked whine and whizzing sound of flying shrapnel pieces let you know how potent a weapon they were. I looked them over carefully; even took one apart, removing the fuse and detonator assembly from the body. I wanted to see what kind of explosive was inside. (This knowledge was valuable later!) It was a granular type of gunpowder. I poured it out, reassembled it and kept this one for a souvenir. Later, I lost it somehow.

On our next adventure, we came across a German ammo dump. A wrecked, burned out truck and tank caught our attention in this field. Fortunately, it was early in the morning and dew was on the grass. A horse and cow had made tracks, wandering around. We wisely stayed in their tracks since we saw round spots here and there where the grass was lighter, suspecting mines had been planted there. We eased over to the tank, being cautious for trip-wires and suspicious for any booby-traps. Looked inside and saw a shiny Luger pistol inside. Ha! This surely was bait! (I gave thanks that as a farm boy I had learned about setting traps for animals).

Nearby, we came upon a big stack of wooden boxes. Must've been a tractor trailer load. After several minutes of careful inspection, we opened one and found they were full of German "potato-masher" grenades. We were itching to throw some, but knew the Germans sometimes could remove the delay-train out of the fuse assembly. While we were trying to figure out how to safely explode one, a man in uniform approached (appeared to be English). We explained our dilemma. He said, "Give me one," and we scattered in a hurry as he threw it. It turned out to be okay, with the normal 5-second delay until it exploded.

Then, we all pitched in and had fun throwing and watching these grenades explode. The horse and cow looked up for a moment and then, nonplussed, went back to eating. Looking around later we ran across a dump truck load of yellow 2" cubes with a hole through the middle. We were tempted to get behind a hedge-row about 100 feet away and throw a grenade on this pile of stuff to see what would happen. Lucky for us the Limey was along. He said they were nitro-starch blocks and the blast would certainly have killed us!

Realizing that we might run into some German stragglers on our forays, and that our 45's weren't that effective as a deterrent, we soon found German rifles and ammo and took these along for protection. Our C.O. found out that many of the men did likewise and ordered all weapons turned in and chewed us out royally.

Lt. Coyne, our bombardier, at one of the base's 50 caliber air raid defense machine guns. Photo taken at A-26, France.

2September, 4314, Went up flying for instrument flight test. Passed okay. This would be necessary for flying in bad weather.

5September, 4123, 4X1000, Gun emplacements at Fort Brest, France. Saw bombs hit and the explosion caused shock wave rings in the cool moist morning air. Like dropping a pebble in a still pool of water. From the smoke down there, there was a lot of heavy fighting going on in the area.

Chapter 13

A-41 Field, Normandy: 50th mission R and R

15 September, moved from A-26 to A-41 at Dreux, France. When we arrived at A-41, Dreux Field, we got our first close look at wrecked German planes. We had apparently bombed and strafed this place. There were broken and burned fighters, bombers and transports all around the edge of the field. Hangars and other buildings were shattered and leveled or burned. Visible patches in the runway indicated that it had been cratered.

We erected pup tents and slept on the ground. We had only "K" rations to eat. By now, most of my clothes were dirty and I'd not had a bath since we departed England. Fortunately we learned the local French ladies would do your laundry, if you'd give them a big bar of G.I. soap. I quickly secured some soap and made contact with a local woman who seemed quite happy to do my laundry. Next, there was a small stream nearby and a bunch of us decided we'd go down and wash up. The stream was about 50 feet across and deep. We stripped, stood on the rocks on the shore and soaped up…water was cold. Finally, we figured we'd jump in for a rinse and swim. I dove in and found that inasmuch as the surface water was cold, at depth it was like ice. I hastily made shore and clambered out, blue and shivering. That water must have been runoff from the Alps! Later on that day, we came across the local ladies washing clothes at the stream further down. They'd dip clothes in the water, lay it on a rock, take a swipe at it with the bar of soap and then scrub the hell out of it with a big brush.

General Eisenhower visited us. Our C.O. rented a hall and arranged for caterers, planning a big affair. When Ike saw our circumstances, he snubbed our C.O. and ate K-rations off the hood of his jeep. He then spent a couple of hours talking with us lower ranked troops. Our opinion of him rose tremendously.

I had a replacement pilot tenting next to me. He didn't smoke, drink, cuss or mess with women; always studied his officers' manual and often read the bible. Golly. What a guy! Figured he'd really go places some day. After a couple of missions, he disappeared; later learned he got sent home due to battle fatigue.

17September, 4314, 4X1000, Enskirchen, Germany, weather wicked with big thick clouds.

18September, 4314. Flew from A-41 to A-15 for an overnight stay as Don visited his brother in the infantry. I stayed with the plane to guard it and the next day we returned to A-41.

20September, 4314, 28X100, Railroad yard at Trier, Germany. On return, in the late afternoon, the shadows of WWI trenches in the low sun were visible below as we passed east of Paris.

A very pretty sight. This was about my 50th mission.

22September, 158. Made a cross-country flight from A-41 to Hesden Field, England. We landed, then took off and returned to A-41. However, by the time I got back, the sun had gone down and it was dark. Couldn't use radio and our field couldn't turn the runway lights on. I really don't know to this day how I ever found the field. As I came in on approach, I turned my landing lights on as I got low and found I was off to the right of the runway. No problem; I quickly made an "S" turn to the left and landed okay.

27September, Left for England for a seven-day R&R leave. Stangle and the rest of the crew went to Scotland.

On my 50th mission R&R, I could pick where I wanted to go. I decided to go to Blackpool…England's Atlantic City. I flew to England and rendezvoused with an English nurse I'd got to know and we took the train to our destination. The ride was relaxing. After securing a room near the beach, we began exploring. I spent a lot of time just walking on the beach, watching the waves and the seabirds. We could hear the waves crashing on the shore at night. This sound was like heaven. We went to the local concert hall and enjoyed the music there. The theatre presented a wonderful play with very good actors who seemed very professional. Many little restaurants offered reasonable fare; we ate a lot of fish and chips. There was an amusement park area and we tried the bigger rides. They were thrillers!

Probably we just enjoyed being together, talking about God, life and a more perfect world. Whether sitting quietly holding hands or strolling hand-in-hand barefooted in the sand, being with an intelligent, sensitive and compassionate companion healed many invisible wounds. Togetherness chased one's fears and cares away. We seemed to draw courage from each other. When it came time to return and part, a new brave resolve came to us, to continue on in our fight to make the world a better and happier place.

Chapter 14

A-72 Field, Mons en Chasse: Getting to Know the French

7 October, 4314. Moved from A-41 to A-72, Mons en Chasse, France. It had nice concrete runways. We'd stay here for about six months. This was my last flight with my first crew pilot, Captain Don Stangle. A wonderful pilot and a good man! Don's West Point training made him a strict disciplinarian, but our working together benefited me tremendously later. I was promoted to First Lieutenant.

Our move to A-72 at Peronne, France was a relief. The Germans had occupied this field before us. Whether they or the French had built it, I never determined. It too had been bombed, but other than a few craters, not much damage was visible. There remained a large brick building which we used for briefings and a group of prefab wood buildings where most of us were housed. Quite a few people lived in larger pyramid tents; some were elaborately added to, using scrap wood to construct solid floors and walls.

This was more livable, resembling our facilities at the English bases. We had a separate mess hall and latrines enough so that it was convenient for everyone. The lavatories here were different; instead of commodes, there was a three foot square porcelain fixture sunk in the floor with two raised foot shaped pedestals to squat on (with a hole, appropriately placed). Instead of individual sinks, there was a common trough with faucets. But best of all, there was a shower and most of the time, hot water!

The wood barracks were about 30' X 100', with a hallway through, lengthwise, and four rooms on each side, approximately 12' X 24' in size. I recall there were about four to six men to a room. We had metal beds and down sleeping bags. On the first night, I saw a big, grey louse crawling down the wall. I jumped up and got out the DDT powder and promptly doused myself, the bed and my sleeping bag thoroughly and went back to sleep. Luckily, I never was bothered by the pests in all of my stay there.

Apparently, the local people and our mess officer made some arrangements. During winter, it was very cold and the snow got deep, and the local French were suffering a food shortage. Garbage cans were placed outside; when we were through eating, leftovers were deposited in the cans. A line of French women and children with containers would form and each would reach in and salvage morsels to take home, some eating them as they walked away. Sad to say, in society there always seems to be a few mean spirited, sadistic individuals. A few fellows seemed to delight in mashing cigarettes in their leftovers and dumping full canteen cups of coffee into the garbage can. This malicious, insensitive behavior filled me with disgust. It saddened me immensely to realize that perhaps a few of us forgot that we were officers and gentlemen. In addition, we had our American traditions to uphold!

At every opportunity, we acquired G.I. soap and soon I found a local woman to do my laundry. She was doing the laundry for everyone in our barracks, I think. Her husband and three children would walk one-half mile across the field through the snow to pick up and return the clothes. There was a boy of 12, a girl 9 and one 6 years old. They were all poorly dressed and the kids sometimes had rags tied around their feet. One of our men discovered that they had no shoes. Seeing the kids limp one day, one fellow took them to our dispensary. The Corpsman found black spots on their feet from having been frozen. Immediately, guys with kids about the same size wrote home and asked for shoes and stockings. I believe around Christmas, the goodies came. When given the shoes and socks, the kids laughed and cried and hugged us, all at the same time. I gave the husband a pair of German boots I'd found when I was in Germany. Boy! He was as happy and proud as a peacock.

The lady baked a cake for us (it wasn't too good). Say! We thanked her, hugged and kissed her on the cheek and wolfed it down, pretending it was the greatest. She was so happy. There was a local dance one night and the family invited me to come. It was held in an old schoolhouse, not too big. The musicians played a tune which had a beat like a polka. I got to dance a few times with different ladies; quite polite and respectful, but friendly. The music and dancing were old traditional French folklore and I really enjoyed it.

On the way back to camp, they invited me to stop at their home. They thanked me for coming, apologized for not having any coffee and I reciprocated, expressing my feelings as best I could in my limited French vocabulary. I was shocked to find the inside of the home strung with clotheslines everywhere, loaded with wet clothes. There was little (if any) heat and I couldn't see any sign of a stove. After that experience, I bought gifts for the kids and often found excuses to give them money; she'd sew on buttons or mend a seam. We all, in our hearts, adopted them and tried to help out as we could.

Once a week, a truck or two would take a load of guys into the city of St. Quentin, about 25 miles away. I remember we went in after lunch and were returned by the evening meal. I missed the truck one night and had to walk back to camp because I was scheduled to fly a mission the next day. Didn't get back to camp until around four in the morning. I wore holes in both my shoes, and didn't meet a soul all the way back to base. I had a quick nap and then, up and at 'em! It was fortunate I missed the truck. At camp that morning, I found a lot of fellows in and coming out of the latrine. Everyone had been up all night with a bad case of the G.I.'s. I was glad I missed supper.

St. Quentin was an R&R town for us and the local Army units. The west half of town was off limits; the German's had used the town for their R&R too. Some of the French had apparently become collaborators. No doubt the French Resistance had identified the west side with German sympathizing groups. I got an insight into this by a chance occurrence, which will figure in my story later in March of '44.

One day, during winter, after a heavy snowstorm, when plows had five foot banks of snow on the sides of our runways, we had a B-17 flying fortress make an emergency landing at our field. It made a poor landing, lost directional control, went left through the snow bank (missing two bomb craters), turned and came back through the snow bank onto the runway and finally stayed there. But she just couldn't stop. The hydraulic system no doubt was shot out. Just short of the end of the runway, emergency air-braking system was activated, locking main gear wheels and stood the plane on her nose. Looked like she was going over on her back, but she settled upright. There was a gaping six-foot hole in the left side of the fuselage. We learned that the pilot and copilot had been killed or badly wounded and the engineer had made the landing. After seeing that, we figured that the B-17 was one rugged ship, maybe almost as tough as our B-26!

Many times, when I couldn't get into town and the weather wasn't too bad, I'd ease over to the ordinance officer's tent and beg a handful of 45 ammo. Then, I'd take a hike out into the countryside and do some shooting, practicing my pistol marksmanship. I was getting more accurate with my pistol and had confidence in my ability to put up a fierce defense, if necessary. Carried my pistol in a shoulder holster, tied down securely, with five clips of ammo (giving me 35 shots at survival!). Learning of some of the experiences of pilots who'd been shot down and escaped, I also knew that sometimes a big knife was a better weapon, under certain circumstances. I wrote my Dad of my needs and he had one made and sent it to me. It had an eight-inch blade and was just right; I strapped it to my leg when I flew missions.

Chapter 15

I am First Pilot with My Own Crew: Bombing the German Homeland

12 October, I was notified that I was now rated "first pilot unlimited." About this time, I'd flown the required number of missions to go back to the USA. I'd decided that, if I could, I'd rather stay here with the 397th, flying B-26's. I knew it would be probable that shortly after I got home, they'd assign me to a new bomber group with B-29's and send me over into the Pacific war zone. I wanted not to get flying over vast expanses of water again. So, I asked my C.O. if I could stay over for a second tour in the European Theatre of Operations with him and he said, "Okay." I stayed until the war ended in Europe.

20October, 4117, (I am Pilot; hereafter, I will note this as "RMC Pilot") II C 5, 4X1000, 2:50, Lt. "Porky" Borgstrom was my co-pilot. We hit a railroad bridge in Gertautdenberg, Germany. Bombs were dropped by pathfinder, lots of thick clouds. I got to do a lot of formation flying in clouds, which severely limit visibility, so that sometimes, the plane you are flying over is nothing more than a vague shadow. This is very stressful, rough and horrifying!

29October, 4123, Porky Pilot, 2:00. Window-dropped tinsel (metallic strips) to fool enemy radar into believing our bomber formation was located where the tinsel was scattered. We spread it out, down below the main group so enemy flak shells would explode a safe distance under them.

4November, 4129, RMC Pilot, 4X1000, 2:30, Baumholder, Germany.

10November, 4314, Porky Pilot, 16X250, 1:35. Horrible weather conditions.

18November, 4123, RMC Pilot, I C 3, 16X250, 3:00, Ammo dump in Rickenbach, Germany, Porky co-pilot, intense accurate flak. This was a rough one.

21November, 161, Porky Pilot, 2:00, Spreading-window over Bergstein, Germany, light accurate flak. I was the co-pilot on this one and also acted as navigator. Did an excellent job.

1December, 4128, RMC Pilot, II B 6, 16X250, 2:40, Saarlautern, Germany. Lots of icing in the clouds; had a rough flight.

5December, 161, RMC Pilot, 16X250, 2:40, Fuel dump at Stammelin, Germany. Hit bullseye with moderate accurate flak. Lt. North led our flight (on his last, 55th mission) and did one of the best, smoothest jobs I'd seen yet. It was minus 20 degrees up there and the boys in the back almost froze!

6December, 136, RMC pilot, 16X250, 2:20, Fuel and ammo dump near Nideggen, Germany. Flattened target good. Light accurate flak.

8December, 4128, RMC Pilot, 16X250, 3:20, Pathfinder mission through clouds over Losheim, Germany. Wicked weather again, with lead planes on instruments; this is not fun!

9December, 4117, 2:25, Pathfinder mission (spreading chaff) over Weisbach, Germany. Porky pilot on this one, flying his last mission. Intense inaccurate flak below us. We'd had lots of fun together.

10December, I got a 48-hour pass to Paris for R&R. I had a real tub bath at a nice hotel and had a very good time there.

15December, 222, 16X250, II A 4, 4:00, Oil storage depot at Ruthen, Germany, no flak or fighters. From this date I will be the pilot on all missions.

Chapter 16

Rescuing the Boys at the Buldge: The Beginning of the End

23 December, Weather had grounded us. This is the first day we could fly to help the Bastone "Bulge" boys. I didn't go up but my first crew pilot, Captain Don Stangle did. He got shot down by fighters, survived crash landing, but was killed by civilians on the ground that they had surrendered to. I didn't learn about Don's death for some time but when I did, it was a hard blow. We had bonded and became buddies…but life goes on.

The Nazi FW-190 and ME-109 fighters numbered about 35 and they shot down 10 or 11 of our planes—60-70 men, that hurt! We had about 36 on that mission. Later I learned the details about that day. I've thought about it a lot, and I think it should not have happened. There were two causes: First, I understand we were to have fighter escort planes to join us, to protect us…they never showed up. Our boys had to continue without them. Second, I learned from some of the flying crew members that only one machine-gun in ten worked that day, the others malfunctioned or didn't function at all.

I remember when we started combat operations from England, when we got out over the Channel, all the guys in the back of the plane would load and fire a few rounds from their guns. This was good, as they gained confidence knowing their guns worked okay. One day, some bullets and some empty fired cartridge cases, accidentally hit other planes in the formation. Our C.O. ordered that there would no longer be any test firing of the guns. They should only be shot if we were attacked.

Well, knowing human nature, if you don't shoot a gun, it's not dirty so you don't have to clean it. Consequently, over many months, the guns got gummed up, corroded and accumulated lots of airborne dust and grit. A few gunners were conscientious no doubt and cleaned and checked their guns periodically, but most did not.

Other groups, I learned, had similar problems but took remedial action to solve this problem. It was a shame that apparently our C.O. didn't contact the other C.O.'s for advice.

We were the last group to go over to England. One expects one's C.O. to be experienced and capable of making wise decisions. I think the boys knew they bore a risk when we proceeded without fighter escorts, but due to the urgency of that mission, I think they should be excused. However, the fact that the boy's guns malfunctioned is inexcusable. This left them defenseless. This shouldn't have happened!

24December, 141, RMC Pilot, II B 6, 2X2000, 3:05, Railroad tunnel at Nideggen, Germany. An Army Brigdier General was in

#4 position in a plane piloted by Col. McLoed, C.O. of the 596th Squadron. We had to make three bomb runs before our bombardier could get it just right and hit it good. This got to be hard work. Thankfully, there was no flak or fighters.

25December, 191, II B 4, 28X100, 3:30, At Ahrdorf, Germany. We hit a hornets' nest! Accurate flak for about 25 minutes. When we got back to home field, we couldn't land due to snow storm and low ceiling, poor visibility. We were diverted to Clastre, France, where the 387th bomb group was stationed at A-71. We landed okay. They had room for us and treated us just fine.

This base had barracks set down in excavated areas which were below ground level. I think this was so the Nazi's could put camouflage netting over to conceal them. They put me down in one of them. I slept in some guy's bed who was on leave. These guys had a screened-off section in which four or five young, beautiful models or actresses came that night. I never did find out what was going on. Wow! I think we returned to A-72 the next day. Merry Christmas!

Combat Missions
1945

13January, 4285, 4X1000, 3:30, Highway bridge at Drasburg, Germany, light accurate flak. Flight leader, Lt. Wynn, did a poor job; Lt. George's plane got disabled and he bailed out. It was cold as hell!

16January, 4315, II B 3, 8X500, 2:52, Railroad yards at Erkelenz, Germany. Flight lead by Lt. Kerley was rough, not smooth. This made hard work for me to hold proper position. On returning, I made a bad landing; I seemed to have lost my depth perception, thinking I was about to kiss the ground, when in reality we were still five to six feet in the air. We stalled out, fell down and hit the ground hard. Other than being ashamed and feeling stupid, I was clueless as to why this happened. I've thought about this and think I may have been having a side-effect from the sulfa tablets they gave us for sinusitis.

22January, 4315, I A 3, 2X2000, 4:30, Railroad bridge near Bullay, Germany. Bombed by Pathfinder through clouds and got fair hits. No flak or fighters. On return, A-72 was closed due to another snow storm and we were diverted to Cormeilles on Vexin, France, where the 344th group was at A-59 field. We landed okay. Think we returned the next day.

29January, 4315, 2X2000, 3:50, Railroad bridge at Whittlock, Germany. Hairy weather, cold as hell…our cockpit window frosted over.

Chapter 17

My First Dead-Stick Landing

2 February, 4315, 2X2000, 3:30, Railroad bridge at Konblez, Germany. We got moderate accurate flak at target and unfortunately missed the bridge; with bombs straying into nearby buildings. Right engine went out of control, rapidly backfiring and quitting, then a second later, catching on full throttle, and again and again. Fearing that it might tear away or catch fire, I shut it down and went on single engine.

We couldn't fly as fast, thus we were soon alone. Since we'd been wingman in our flight, we had only a toggeleer in the nose, who dropped our bombs when the lead ship dropped his (bombing by "flights"). Only the flight leader and the deputy flight leader (numbers one and four, respectively) had a bombardier and a navigator. I'd have to do the navigation to get back home. We soon discovered that one of the other flight crews had decided to accompany us; they'd ride shotgun for us to discourage any Nazi fighter pilots looking for an easy kill.

Things went well, until I began to prepare myself for landing with a single engine. We had to transfer gas from our right into our left main. I told the co-pilot, Lt. U.L. Bauer (who I should have been watching more closely) to go back, get engineer and transfer our gas. Apparently they screwed up, because shortly, my left engine began to act up. It quit, caught on, quit, caught on and quit for good. I had to fight to keep the plane under control and got the nose down to maintain flying speed and pick out an emergency landing field (now we had a glider!). I feathered left propeller, cut the switches and we started gliding toward a field. We'd been lowering altitude and I felt it best that we not bail out, but to go in for a belly landing…the field looked plenty big enough.

Looking back to tell crew, I saw only the copilot. I asked, "Where's the crew,?" he said, "They're gone." Apparently when our only engine quit, he reacted reflexively and told the crew to bail out. There was a switch in the bomb bay and that's how they exited the plane. I told the copilot we were going to belly-land and to buckle up! Unfortunately, nobody talks about gliding in a B-26. Generally, they say it flies like a rock, without any power. I thought that wasn't true, but I had no idea what the angle of the glide would be. I had to make a big "S" turn to the right, but I tried to keep the loops small enough to still be flying when we sat down.

It happened that we touched down real smooth…hardly felt it. But we landed a little faster than ideal, because our field had a rise in the middle of it and trees at the end. We slid into a hump, which like a ski-jump threw us up 15 to 20 feet. When we came down, we instantly stopped. The impact was hard; I couldn't breathe and my torso felt like it was on fire. Thought I might die, but then I began to breath and unfastened my seat belt. The copilot seemed okay, so we opened the overhead escape hatches and climbed out.

The plane looked pretty good, except we'd set down with the bomb bay doors open and the plane was full of mud and dirt. The impact wrinkled the rear fuselage and it drooped down somewhat. The propellers and wings seemed undamaged. Our shotgun-riding buddy went to home field and told them what happened and where we were located. It wasn't too long before a rescue team came with an ambulance.

The toggeleer was the first man to bail out, he hadn't adjusted his parachute harness properly and hit the ground stiff-legged. The impact shock caused three vertebras to collapse. A French farmer saw him come down. He went out and picked him up, took him to his house and put him in a bed, mud, boots, and all. When the ambulance team took him away, I went down to see the farmer to thank him and pay him for the dirty bed, but he said, "No, I thank you and all the other Americans who drove those Nazi soldiers away." We sat down and talked and he served some sugar-beet brandy and we became fast friends.

The second man out, my engineer/tail gunner, was still swinging as he came down alongside a barn and swung into the stone wall, knocking him out. When he woke up, he was okay. The third man out landed okay in a field, but before he could collapse his chute, the wind dragged him into a hedgerow and he got bruised and scratched up a bit. The last man, our turret gunner, jumped too low to the ground, and he hit before his chute could open. I learned later that the copilot looked back after he sat down and belted up, saw the boy in the bomb bay and waved him out instead of motioning for him to come up front with us.

I woke up the next morning and I couldn't get out of bed. It hurt to move…I felt like my body was on fire. I didn't know why, because

I didn't have any visible injuries. Then I thought that maybe I had battle fatigue. Good lord, I could not go to the dispensary and let them find out, or they'd send me home and I would be disgraced. So, I told my roommates not to tell anyone. I lay on the bed for four days; on 6Febrary, I was scheduled to fly again. I had to do it. Somehow (every movement was painful), I got dressed, went down for the briefing, picked up my chute and flak vest and got out to the truck to go to my plane. I couldn't climb up into the truck to sit on the bench seats inside, but somehow managed to get up on the tailgate. Out at the plane, I had trouble climbing the ladder to get into the cockpit, but some of the crew gave me a boost in the behind and I was up there okay. I flew the mission alright and never stopped till the war ended.

Above the Clouds

Going out on my first mission, four days after my first dead-stick landing.

6February, 7823, II C 5, 16X250, 2:45, Railroad bridge at Setenich, Germany. Weather was terrible. Big, thick clouds. Flying formation under instrument conditions wasn't fun!

Chapter 18

My Second Dead-Stick Landing

9 February, 7605, I C 5, 8X500 "B", 3:00, Supply depot and ammo dump at Viersen, Germany. Bombs dropped on pathfinder signal. Light accurate flak. Lots of instrument flying in formation – some fun!

14February, 4314, II C 4, 4X1000, 3:15, Railroad bridge at Mayenne, Germany. Made four bomb runs before dropping. Formation-flying bad for everyone, moderate accurate flak.

15February, 4123, I C 4, 4X1000, 3:10, Railroad bridge at Mayenne, Germany. Swenson lead flight just swell. We bombed by box on pathfinder through clouds. Light accurate flak.

23February, 4314, II A 4, 2X2000, 4:00, Supply depot, ammo dump and town fortifications at Jackarath, Germany., Terrible weather...cold as hell, missed target. Got back to home field and found base closed due to heavy snowstorm. Diverted to Reims, France.

One of our flight leaders was scheduled to go to Cannes, France for R&R leave on return (and so was I!). Apparently, he was a determined chap, and he broke formation and went to land. We had no knowledge of this because we could only see no further than 75 to 100 feet. Suddenly, a six-ship flight crossed 50 feet below us at about 60 degrees to our course. This was a near catastrophe. I don't know if he and his flight made a safe landing or not, but my guardian angel was sure on the job!

When we got to Reims, they only had ½ mile visibility and a 200 foot ceiling, I was told later. When it came time for us to land, we were the fourth flight and it was quite dark. On my flight, I was the fourth ship. We had to separate to establish a safe time interval of at least 30 seconds. Turning onto my approach, I couldn't see anything. When I got down to what I thought was 500 feet, I turned on my landing lights. All I saw was some trees and a hill on my right. Then, I saw a runway, but it was angled 40 degrees off what it should've been. I quickly lined up and landed. At the end of the runway, I turned off and shut off my landing lights. Another plane came in after me, but either he had landing gear failure or forgot to put his wheels down, sparks started flying as soon as he hit the tarmac. He caught on fire but I think he slid off on the grass to the right of the runway.

It turned out that this was an auxiliary field near Reims and had no permanent personnel. There were no fire trucks or rescue teams. After a while, some people from the Reims air field showed up and transported us to a big tent. There were cots, G.I. sleeping bags, K-rations and there was a big puddle of water in the middle of the tent. I nearly froze to death; kept waking up shivering. Rough night.

25February, 4314, I C 1, 8X500 "B", Railroad bridge near Greivonboich, Germany. We took off with a thick, heavy overcast of clouds and a low ceiling. We've developed a technique for these conditions: the individual flights of six form up under the clouds, as they circuit the field. The flight leader leads his flight on a designated course, at a fixed speed and a fixed rate of climb on instruments, up through the clouds until they break out on top. They circle, and as the others following in trail come, they form their boxes and proceed on their mission.

Visibility varies in clouds from an estimated 100 to 150 feet. Our right wingman, apparently inexperienced and not tucked in tight, lost sight of us shortly after we got into the clouds. Suddenly, I heard a loud roar of a B-26 and saw the belly of one right at my wingtip. Once again, my guardian angel was with me!

At the target, the snow on the ground made identification of the bridge difficult, and we had to make two runs before our bombardier dropped the bombs. This separated us from the main group, but I could still see them. I increased speed to join up with them. Inadvertently, we passed over and enemy 88mm AAA site, and they were good shots. They made a direct hit on my tail. The shell exploded as it hit, blowing a big hole in my right stabilizer-elevator assembly, causing it to fold up, twist and break away. When this occurred, my plane yawed hard right and it was just like my right engine was killed. Reflexively, I shut it down and feathered the propeller. Up until then, I didn't know for sure how badly we were damaged. Then the tail gunner came into the cockpit white-faced and said, "They blew the whole tail off!" I knew that wasn't accurate since I was still able to wag my wings to let my flight know I was leaving. I had to start evasive action, and knowing the enemy aimed at the lead plane, I'd draw fire away from the flight. I called the top turret-gunner and he told me about the right stabilizer-elevator being shot away; he evidently didn't see that about half of my rudder was blown away too. Its trim tab didn't help, and I had to hold full left rudder...had to ask my copilot to get on his left rudder pedal too, to help me. The flak suddenly stopped.

A photo of my damaged tail. The Marauder is one tough bird.

Above the Clouds

We couldn't maintain altitude at a safe speed, so I had to gradually lose altitude. A P-47 fighter appeared off our left wing. He stayed with us until we got back into safe territory. A cloud slid under us, and I had to descend on instruments through it. I decided we must lighten the plane, so I told the crew to throw out everything that was loose. That did it! We could maintain altitude, but we were down to around 2,000 feet. Our navigator brought us back to A-72. I wasn't about to try to make my first single-engine landing with only half a tail on my plane. I'd been frantically thinking of how to get my wonderful crew and this beautiful plane down on the runway safely. I'd seen lots of damaged ships come in, lose control and crack up, some burning. I suddenly remembered one of the older experienced combat pilots advising me that one ought to fly a damaged plane in to where you can get it in with no power, before you cut the power.

So, I flew in to about 30 degrees to the end of the runway before I dropped my landing gear. When it locked it down, I cut my engine and feathered my propeller as I started my glide with no flaps. I'd planned to round out fast to be sure my limited tail surfaces would maintain control. Worked great so far, now we were floating down the runway like a glider...but she wouldn't slow down! The landing area was shrinking fast. In desperation, I flew it down onto the runway, but before I could get the brakes to take, she flew up. I'd forgotten that the attack angle on the "G" model B-26's wing had been increased; the older "C" model would have stayed down. With the runway getting dangerously short, I prayed and stayed on the brakes. I sat her down again. The landing gear took this abuse in stride. We stopped okay, with a little runway to spare. I think we all thanked God as we exited the ship, rather humbled. I learned later that there was nothing wrong with our right engine. And I

Major Richard M. Crummett

still wonder if that P-47 had one of our boys flying it or was there a Nazi pilot in one they had fixed up from some that got shot down?

Chapter 19

Nightmarish Practical Joke

The new replacement pilots apparently heard stories about me and decided they would test me, while disbelievers would hope to show me up as just an ordinary guy, or worse, prove me a coward. They set up a trap secretly and caught me by surprise, completely unsuspecting.

I was seated at my bunk one night, trying to concentrate on writing a letter. A bunch of guys were coming and going, and a group was sitting on a bunk across from me. My consciousness had just begun to pick up the words "wonder how it works," when I heard a familiar "pop" and "hiss" sound, just like our "pineapple" fragmentation grenade, when activated. Looking where the sound came from revealed a man with one of these grenades in his hand, sitting on a bunk ten feet away—directly across from me.

The next thing I knew, I was standing in the center of the room, with everyone behind me. I had the body of the grenade clutched tightly to my stomach in my right hand. In my left hand, I had unscrewed the fuse/detonator assembly. My brain screamed, "Toss it before it blows your fingers off!" I threw it into the now vacant corner of the room where my bed was. It hit the wall, fell and exploded before it landed.

Suddenly, an adrenalin rush hit me. I became weak, shaken and staggered over to my bed and sat down. As I did, my peripheral vision caught a fleeting glimpse of the group of fellows who had the grenade, running out of the room. (I never did find out their identity. My roommates, now probably deceased, didn't know who they were). As my heartbeat began to get back to normal, I found myself still clutching the grenade body in my right hand. I tilted it over to pour out the explosive charge, so I could dispose of it safely. Nothing came out—it was empty!

I'm proud of how I reacted to this threat. No doubt my having taken one apart at A-26 helped. Also, our training in preparation for a possible Nazi paratrooper attack broadened our awareness of unusual situations. I'm glad this wasn't a German "potato masher" grenade. I'd taken one of these apart too, back at A-26. You can't unscrew the handle to disarm one in three seconds. You'd have to throw your body on top of it, to save your buddies. The handle joined the body with a set of fine threads. It took many turns to unscrew and separate the handle/fuse and detonator assembly from the explosive section, the main body.

My choices were limited. Our windows were covered with pup tent halves and boards.

Our barracks had a central aisle, with rooms on each side. Our room was in the central part, so you couldn't have thrown it out the door. Anyway, after this happened, the new replacement pilots seemed to become more friendly and respectful of this older (experience-wise) Marauder pilot!

Chapter 20

A Bout of Anoxia

27 February, 4323, II C 1, 4X1000, 3:15, Railroad repair and storage buildings at Ahrweiler, Germany. We bombed by pathfinder. It was bitter cold, and we got lots of icing in the clouds. They took our de-icing boots off our wings because they said we wouldn't need them! We did lots of instrument flying through the dense clouds.

28February, 7864, II C 1, 4X1000, Railroad bridge at Mayenne, Germany. A milk run!

1March, 4158, II B 1, 8X500 on "Gee" at Pulheim, Germany. Lt. Wynn in lead box; bombed by boxes, rough one…not smooth! F.U.B.A.R.

4March, 4323, 3:00, Lead of three-ship window element at Bruhl, Germany. Group bombed by pathfinder through the clouds. Bottom ceiling was at 1000 feet. The top got higher as we got near the target, requiring us to get up above 14,000 feet…and we had no oxygen or heat; they took them out because they said we wouldn't need 'em! It was cold as the devil and our sheepskin pants, jackets and helmets were left behind in England because, you guessed it, we wouldn't need them anymore. We got rime and clear ice on the plane going to the target and it was the same going back to base.

Our position prior to getting to the target was to be to the right and about 500 feet above the highest flight of the second box. Up there for a relatively long time, I developed anoxia (low blood oxygen). Everything seemed fine, but I was mentally impaired. You feel fine and are unaware of what is happening. Just before reaching the target, I and my two wingmen would dive down under the lead box, to get out in front, zigzagging back and forth as we spread our "chaff" like a big blanket below the lead box to fool enemy into thinking that they were down there. As we were spreading chaff, a cloud seemed to rise up like an ocean wave in front of me. We hit it and I expected to pop out in a couple of seconds. We didn't and I was puzzled. I had started flying instruments as soon as we hit the cloud and it appeared that everything was alright. All of a sudden, my copilot, Jim Voelker, slapped my right shoulder and pointed to my turn-and-bank indicator. It took a couple of seconds to realize that we were in a diving spiral! My bombardier and navigator later told me that they thought we were in a spin.

By now, at a lower altitude, my blood-oxygen level improved. I got the plane out of the spiral and dive quickly and climbed up as fast as I could, on the course I knew the group was on. We popped out of the clouds all of a sudden and found ourselves under the bomber formation…they had their bomb-bay doors open! Hey! We made a 90 degree turn, put on full power and got the hell out of there. Luckily, we got out from under before the bombs came raining down. Coming home was rough, cold with icing and instrument flying. But that's just another day's work for us fly boys.

9March, 8086, II C 1, 8X500, 4:00, Factory loading explosives into 88mm artillery shells at Lunen, Germany. Box bombing through clouds by pathfinder with moderate flak. Lots of instrument time; formation in clouds. This trip was a long one.

10March, 8086, 2:50, Railroad and road intersections at Altenkirchen, Germany. Leader of "window" chaff element, box bombing through clouds by pathfinder. The weather was horrible. Plane iced up in the clouds. We flew the usual instrument and formation flying in the clouds routine that we're getting used to by now.

Chapter 21

1st Army Adventure

12 March, Our crew was sent for ten days to the 1st Army. The Army and Air Force had accidents; inadvertently at times, we had each killed some of our own troops. To help remedy this situation, the two forces began an exchange program. We'd send some flight crews up to the front lines and they'd send some of their people back to our bases to live and fly with us awhile.

My crew went to the 1st Army for ten days. We took two jeeps because there were seven of us in the crew. I had two men with me and the copilot had three. The ride took longer than anyone had anticipated and finally, we got lost. We'd only been given the password to cover us for one day. By midnight, we still hadn't reached the 1st Army HQ and we were getting anxious. We didn't know the password for the next day. With only our blackout lights on (like candles in the dark!), we were putting along in second gear when suddenly a spotlight hit us…we stopped in a hurry. Out of the corner of my eye I saw a soldier covering us with a Tompson submachine gun and, speaking softly, cautioned my guys to freeze. We were spoken to in French; we'd run into a French unit. I explained that we were Americans and finally, someone who spoke English arrived and we explained our circumstances and our destination. We got directions and finally found the 1st Army HQ.

Immediately, as we stopped at the guard booth, we were surrounded by soldiers with M-1 rifles with fixed bayonets. We were marched in to be interrogated. Boy! I couldn't answer many of the questions about famous sports figures, etc. and began to get worried. I knew that some German troops had infiltrated our line and were wearing American uniforms, driving our vehicles, too. At long last, partly in exasperation, our interrogating officer said, "Hell, you guys must be Americans, 'cause the Germans would know all the answers!" and we were released.

We reported to some General the next morning and were assigned to our units. We were split up; going where the action was. We could not go below battalion level in the combat area. Since we would be separating, my copilot and I agreed to meet at Liege, Belgium on the way back to base.

Anyway, being around HQ was sort of a nightmare. With all the Generals going here and there and the guards and sentries popping to attention whenever one passed, scared the heck out of us.

The Division passed us down to Brigade and finally to Battalion HQ. To reach our Battalion, we had to cross the Rheine River at Remagen. They were located out in a pocket one mile deep and three miles wide, on the other side. The railroad bridge was still up, but damaged. German bombers came several times a day and tried to hit it. We crossed the river on a pontoon bridge our engineers had put in place (this could hold a tank). Once across, I pulled over, walked down to the river and pissed in it. I couldn't resist!

There were no siren-warnings, when the anti-aircraft guns opened up, you stopped and dove for cover. One unfortunate time, I pulled into a ditch and dove out, not noticing a 40mm cannon set up alongside on the bank. Wow. When he fired it, it nearly lifted you off the ground! We weren't used to so much loud noise such as this. Another time, we were in town when the guns started, so we pulled onto the sidewalk close to a building and dove inside. The bomb hit a block away but we got showered with debris and falling plaster. When the guns stopped, we went out and as we were getting in the jeep, some General stopped his jeep alongside us and gave me holy hell. He told me never to block a street like that again and to get in our jeep and get out of there pronto. I managed a quick salute and a humble, "Yes, sir!" and quickly obeyed.

To exit the town, we had to pass where the bomb hit. It struck right in the square, where an anti-aircraft gun had been. Nothing left now but a crater and a burning wrecked truck. Passing through an underpass on the other side of the square, I saw a big, red splotch on the wall and looking down, saw half a soldier, split exactly from head to crotch (by a bomb fragment, no doubt), lying there with the exposed, bloody side up. You have no time for emotions…the M.P.'s shouted at us to keep moving, since gas from the truck was running down the hill toward a house with dynamite in it!

Finally, we were getting somewhat used to bombers coming over. We stopped by the side of the road and watched as a cone of tracers reached up to an ME-262 jet, with the apex of the cone behind, never quite catching up to the streaking plane. As I am standing there watching the show, a G.I. standing in a doorway yelled at me to get under cover. Just then I heard a "Whack" sound and looked around and saw a 50 caliber bullet sticking up in the surface of the road. I got the message…what goes up must come down, and dived into the house.

One night, sleeping on a cot in a schoolhouse used as battalion HQ, we experienced our first artillery serenade. About one or two in the morning, we heard a loud explosion, felt the blast and the room lit up with the flash. As I am trying to figure out what happened, more blasts followed in quick succession, with no pause or let-up. I eased over to the window and saw what seemed to be 100 guns (105mm Howitzers) flashing all over the valley floor behind us. One battery of guns was close to and behind the schoolhouse. They continued firing for an hour or two. I later learned that a German tank unit had penetrated our defense line. Our infantry couldn't do much in the dark, so they just kept down in foxholes and called back to HQ to report it. As soon as the tanks got through the line and in the clear in a rear area, we hit them with artillery and destroyed them; this was pretty smart!

We were given a guide one day who was one of only two men surviving from the original outfit which landed in North Africa. He was to go with us and take us up closer where we could observe some action. We went up a hill and into a big gravel pit. At the bottom of the pit, several 80mm mortars were set up. The soldiers had small rock walls erected in coffin-shapes for protection in the event they were fired upon. We climbed the one side and peered over, being cautioned to keep as low as possible, to avoid being spotted. In front of us we could see squads of our infantry advancing, attacking a town on the far hill, about ¾ of a mile away.

Boy! We had a ringside seat. One squad got careless and blundered into a German machine gun; they scattered like a covey of quail! About then our guide yelled at us to get our heads down. The mortars fired some shells while we were up there and each made a sort of "Whissst" sound as they went over our heads. It wasn't

Above the Clouds

long before we heard our first incoming artillery shell. It hit the far wall of the gravel pit. Our guide said that we'd been spotted and it was time to leave. We hesitated. Our thinking was that the troops below would think us Air Corps types as being cowardly. A second shell landed closer; our guide said he was leaving and scrambled down the bank. We still hesitated and a third shell landed closer. I felt a blow on my butt like someone had hit me with a hammer, and bits of rock and dirt rained on us. I reached around and touched my hip...it was wet. God! I thought I'd been hit, but as I looked at my hand, I saw it wasn't red. A quick look revealed the top of my canteen was gone. It was time to leave!

We ran down the bank and as we reached bottom, a shell exploded on the edge of the bank where we had been. They were good; they kept putting shells right where we had been previously, chasing us all the way out of the gravel pit.

I reckon those mortar crews cussed us good. The sound of shells bursting on the ground next to you is pretty terrible. Not only is it loud, but you feel the blast, smell the smoke and the whine of that shrapnel is wicked. One thing amazed me, when you heard and incoming shell, while running, you could dive flat on the floor of a gravel pit amongst rocks the size of grapefruits and not feel any pain, or get hurt! As we got to our jeep, an infantryman asked us to hitch a ride; he'd been shot in the arm. He bitched a lot, but not because he got hit, but rather because the S.O.B. that shot him hadn't hit bone. This was a ticket stateside.

Our guide took us to another battalion command post, again, a schoolhouse. I talked with an infantry captain company commander, trying to get him to take me along on an upcoming attack. He refused; told me that this town on the next hill was heavily defended and was going to be a tough one. Later that afternoon, he was killed as he kicked in a door on an apparently unoccupied house…they cut him in half. Some mortar shells exploded in the field near the school. Damn! They're bad. They don't make a sound coming in, and I didn't know what happened until I was told.

The commander figured there was a German spotter in a water tower in the next town and called in 155mm artillery fire on it. We watched in fascination as with the third round, they hit it. Predictably, as the second round hit, two men came racing out of the tower with their hands held high over their heads. One problem: we couldn't yet determine which shells were ours and which were theirs. We were becoming rather gun-shy about the sound of artillery shells. Guess I was sort of jumpy, by now!

The next day we visited some artillery units. We watched some 105mm Howitzers load and fire. They were firing "indirect fire" and explained. I'd never heard of that before. The flash, the muzzle blast and the noise is something to see and experience. We visited an eight inch Howitzer later. They didn't get any calls to fire, so we didn't get to see what that one was like. I asked them about "direct fire". Could they hit a tank if one appeared? They said they could, provided they had time to load and told me a story. Seems when they first got there and set up, there were still German troops on the other side of the river. Although they were far away, from their hillside position, they had a direct line of sight and could observe what went on over there with binoculars. They're allowed a few rounds to zero in the gun, and they had fired all but one. Then, a German soldier on a bicycle was coming down the road on the other side, pedaling furiously. They decided to try to get him. After some fast calculation, they aimed, fired and the soldier disappeared. We thanked God these guys were on our side!

We got to go to an artillery fire control center. This was also in a schoolhouse. We saw maps showing fields of fire of each battery and how they overlapped. They explained how they planned and coordinated fire missions. While we were there, there was a sudden blast which shook the building and knocked some plaster off the ceiling. Then I heard this in-coming sound. Holy cow. This sounded like the V-2 rockets did in London. I looked out the window and saw a big, smoking hole in the ground about ¼ of a mile away. We drove over and saw some valves pipes, roller chain and pieces of metal, which in my mind confirmed that this had been a V-2. It must have malfunctioned and hit near us, falling short. I believe the crater was 20 feet deep and 50 feet across.

Before leaving, I got to explore a castle south of Remagen, shortly after the infantry passed through the area. It was empty except for some Russian servants about. It had already been looted and was a beautiful place. I looked around and couldn't find anything that I wanted, until in the attic, I found a big pile of paper money in a corner. Grabbed a couple of large denomination bills as souveniers.

Finally, our time was up and we headed for Liege, Belgium. Joining up with the copilot, we learned that they had had closer calls than we did. It was an interesting experience. Wouldn't trade places with the infantry ever. I'll stick to my flying! We were all mighty glad to get back to our home field and start flying again.

CHAPTER 22

DANGEROUS LIAISONS

24 March, 4216, I C 1, 2X2000, 4:35, Bombsight malfunction at target resulted in us bombing a secondary target at Vlotlo-Paderborn, light accurate flak.

One night I'd ridden into town on a motorcycle (my copilot picked it up in Germany when we visited the 1st Army) for fun and adventure. I wound up in a café where nice tender, juicy, thick steak sandwiches were available. While eating and sipping wine, my eye was caught by a beautiful lady at the bar, surrounded by eight or ten Army officers and war correspondents. Her glance was inviting, so I dropped my sandwich and went over to her; not daunted by the superior ranks all around. She brightened up as I approached and accepted my offer to buy her a drink. While waiting for our order, she brushed against me...I could tell she wanted to get out of there, so I invited her for a motorcycle ride. She joyously accepted and we turned and left the café.

As she waited while I started the motorbike, I heard her softly exclaim, "Catastrophe!"

I looked up and here came the Army officers. Hopping clear of the motorcycle, I flipped open the top button of my blouse, gave them as hard a cold stare as I could muster and said, "You gentlemen want anything?" That stopped them cold in their tracks; after a moment's hesitation, they muttered, "No" and turned around and went back into the café. I wasn't armed, but I bluffed them into thinking I might be. Had they known how bad my knees were knocking together, I'd have been beaten badly, no doubt!

Then, I started the motorcycle, she climbed on and we took a ride. We wound up at her place on the west side (forbidden zone) of town. I told her I couldn't park outside, because the M.P.'s might notice. She said I could bring the bike inside. She lived at a large hotel. She went up the steps, opened the big doors and motioned me inside. I drove up the steps and into the lobby and parked.

She introduced me to an older lady who may have been her mother, as she seemed to be scolding my gal and made her sit down and eat some soup. Then she showed me around. There was a big ballroom decorated with beautiful murals painted on the walls. There were scenes of mountains, waterfalls, trees, streams, lakes, deer, birds and lastly, artfully posed nude ladies. Hey! These were my kind of guys. I noted some evidence that the hotel was probably used by the Nazi's, as an officers club. Despite the fact that my esteem of them was raised, they were still my enemy.

We then wasted no time engaging in a prolonged, amorous relationship. During the night, I learned she owned the hotel. Her husband went away with the Nazi's…she didn't know where or even if he might still be alive. She was a survivor. The war brought trouble.

Above the Clouds

They'd tried hard to keep their hotel, not to create any problems, to make a living and not cause anything to happen that would make their friends and neighbors to get hurt. My heart understood. I forgave her. In my heart I felt that it was for God to judge and even he would undoubtedly forgive.

I went back the next day and we found a carnival in town. We went on rides, ate some local food, and I can't remember having more fun. We were like a couple of kids. Everyone was treating her like the mayor, or someone well-liked and respected. They treated me likewise. They all were enjoying themselves…the French are uninhibited when it comes to having fun! Eventually, we'd had enough and returned to the hotel where we resumed our intimate interlude.

She was a beautiful, vivacious, fun-loving lady; our brief time together was a memorable experience. I never had an opportunity to see her again. I became very busy flying no doubt.

3April, 8096, II A 1, 4X1000, 4:30, Railroad storage buildings and yards at Holzminden, Germany. Pathfinder, box-bombing through clouds.

7April, 8096, I B 1, 4X1000, 4:30, Railroad yards at Northein, Germany. Broken clouds caused us to go down from 10,000 feet to 6,200 feet in altitude to get under the clouds, so we could drop our bombs visually. Our camera showed we got excellent hits on target.

9April, 8096, III A 1, 4X1000, 5:30, Manufacturing buildings at Neihagen, Germany. Broken clouds forced us to bomb visually again, from 8,000 feet. Smoke in target area made camera's photos no good, but the bombardier thought we got good hits. We got light accurate flak. By taking evasive action, we kept them from hitting us. After we got back to base, a following flight leader told me I'd had a close call. A German ME-262 jet had popped out of a cloud and was making a run on me, when one of our P-38 escort fighters saw him. He was positioned where he could intercept and shoot down the Nazi jet fighter. The jet pilot saw him and to save his jet, turned away into the clouds. God was with me again!

19April, 8157, III A 1, 2X2000, Railroad yards at Ulm, Germany. Target was obscured by smoke, but we got good hits using surrounding reference points.

20April, 8096, I B 1, 2X2000, Railroad bridge at Gunzberg, Germany. Two flights took off; the third flight leader cracked up on his take-off attempt. Since he caught on fire with bombs aboard, the C. O. shut the airport down. The first flight leader and I had no choice but to leave on the mission. We bombed visually; he hit the first box's target and I hit the second. We were lucky because two flights should have been tempting prey for German fighters. I reckon they knew they were licked, and didn't care anymore.

At St. Quentin's Maison D'Amusements, I met two outstanding Mademoiselles. Most of the girls were skillful; for some it was just a job (their sole means of support). A few were sensitive, compassionate professionals who would open their hearts to you if you treated them with respect, courteousness, praised their beauty, admired their skill and thanked them for their services. One rather young beauty, responding to my question of "What was she doing there?" said, "I'm working to provide a dowry to get married, my family is poor." She was nice. I tipped her heavily. When I approached another lady with the same question, (she was dignified, refined and seemed well-to-do), she responded, "I don't like to ask my husband for extra spending money and I like to get out once in a while, look for a nice guy and the thrills and adventure that come with it." She was a wonderful woman.

CHAPTER 23

Y-55 FIELD, VENLO, HOLLAND: MY NIGHTMARE

25 April, we moved from A-72 field at Mons en Chausse to Y-55 field at Venlo, Holland. This new base was a well camouflaged former German field. We'd never seen anything like this before. It was a beautiful base. The people in the nearby towns weren't cordial toward us at all. Seems they didn't like aviators. I was told by some of the boys, that they chased their young girls into the house; rolled up the sidewalks, and locked up everything early at night...they didn't want to be bothered!

From my diary, I have no record of flying any combat missions from this field. Shortly after we arrived, I was promoted to Captain. Finally got my plane (8096) a name and had nose art painted on. We had the wolf from Little Red Riding Hood painted on with the caption: "Massacre Raiding Marauder". Looked stunning! Never did get a picture of it.

Some night, after our last combat mission and before the war was over, I had a most horrible nightmare. I think it happened because finally, the locker in my brain where I'd been hiding bad and painful things I'd seen and heard (which you must forget, bury or banish from your memory, in order to function and perform your duties) just burst; it couldn't take anymore. Every man in combat, if he survives long enough, eventually reaches his limits and breaks down; everything unloads in condensed form and envelopes him. Anyway, back to the dream.

We were flying along, happy in our plane, everything okay. Suddenly, there's an explosion and momentarily, I am stunned. Something wet has splattered in my face; my copilot's arms are flailing about. I throw my arm over him to keep him from hitting the switches, when I look, and half his head is gone! I try to look out to see what happened to the plane but I can't. The windows are covered in blood that won't wipe off! I will have to fly by our instruments but damn, there's blood gushing out covering them, too. Now I am flying blind and am becoming aware that the blood is gushing out of me. Nobody is there to help me; my copilot has slumped over, probably dead. Maybe the rest of the crew has been killed too!

I can't feel anything with the controls; just like they've been cut…we're out of control for sure. Now we are falling, going down faster and faster, from the sound I am hearing. I don't feel any pain, but I am bleeding to death, (if we don't crash first!). God, I guess it is my time to come home to you. I'd always thought it would be "poof" and I'd be dead, instantly. I never thought getting killed would be like this. Suddenly, we are on fire; I feel the heat and see the flames. A big ball of fire bursts into the cockpit. I am on fire.

Oh, God. It burns so terrible! I don't want to burn to death…and everything stops.

It is silent now; I don't feel any pain, nothing. I am in blackness; I must be dead now. We must have hit the ground. Funny, didn't feel or hear anything when we crashed. Then I sense that I am wet with sweat. I seem to be trembling, shaking and I am breathing hard, like I have just run a mile. Maybe this was how I was at the time of the crash? Why should I feel this now? Who knows what one feels or senses as a spirit? Then, I smell something. This is really strange. Can spirits smell? It seems familiar…hey, that's tarpaper. We had that smell in our barracks at Venlo. A spirit can go anywhere, I guess, so probably I came here, to get back with my buddies.

I don't know how long it took before I began to realize that I was in my bunk in our barracks. Or how long it took for me to accept the fact that I had a nightmare. I don't know if I screamed or hollered, my roommates never said anything.

8May, 3:00 hours, We were awakened by machine-gun fire, when someone came into our barracks and told us the war (European Theatre of Operations) was over.

Chapter 24

17 May, I was told that I could go home. They scheduled me to go to Paris and sent a crew along to bring the ship back home. I had the pilot buzz the fields as we left; he told them that I did it. Well, he buzzed the field pretty good. I should have hugged and kissed that ship as I left, but touch her, I couldn't. I hitched a ride on a C-47 to England. I wound up spending about two months there. I got together with an English nurse I'd been with before and we spent most of our time in Bournemouth, where we'd formerly been based. Finally, I ran out of money and went to one of our U.S. military posts, to pick up my pay. They saw my orders and said, "You're on your way home. We have a plane leaving. Want us to put you on the list?" I said, "Okay" and so I left England.

15July, Arrived at Whorton, England, ready for the final journey home.

17July, Departed Whorton and landed at Valley.

20July, Departed Valley and landed at Prestwick, Scotland (topped off gas tanks).

20July, Departed Prestwick, Scotland for Meeks Field in Iceland. About 45 minutes out, our right engine began to run rough and cut out. We turned back and landed at Stornoway Field in New Hebrides Islands. After repair, we took off again.

20July, Finally made it to Meeks Field, Iceland. Got a good look at the North Atlantic. The ocean was rough, lots of white caps on the waves. As we got close to Iceland, we began to see more and more icebergs, We had never seen Iceland before and were surprised to see no ice or snow! After landing, discovered that the ground was sandy and covered with round stones of varying sizes. This made walking off the paved surfaces difficult.

22July, Departed Meeks Field, Iceland for BW-1 Field in Greenland. Arrived okay. Found Greenland almost totally covered with ice and snow. Our field had been built on the side of a fjord. To land, you had to approach from the ocean. It was like flying into a box canyon. You landed at the water's edge, with a steep mountainous wall of rock ahead.

23July, Departed Greenland and went to Goose Bay, Labrador, Canada. North America looks good, even though it was wild and primitive forest land.

24July, Departed Labrador for Bradley Field in Connecticut. There was nothing but forest below all through Canada and most of the state of Maine. Began to see small towns finally. The farther down we got, the more civilized it appeared. Compared to Europe, where everything is arranged so precisely, neat and clean, America is more or less sloppily laid out. What a contrast!

24July, Home again! Wow, does the U.S.A. look good. Ditto American gals and food! The first thing I did was have a glass of fresh milk. I never dreamed I'd live to come home. Gosh. Where do I go from here?

We checked through customs okay and we were sent home on leave. I took a train up to Waterville, Maine and called home. My dad came down and took me back to the farm. Of course, I'd not called ahead of time to let them know I was back from Europe. I wondered if I had, would there have been a band and a crowd of welcomers?

Epilogue

A couple of months after I got home, an older man, who I got to know and respect, came to talk to me. He said the members of the Masonic Lodge would like to have me join them and become a member. I knew my grandfather had been a Mason, so I said, "Sure. I'd be glad to."

I didn't know anything about the Masonic order, but my grandmother said it was a good organization. After my initiation and finally being raised and accepted as a Master Mason, my grandmother asked if they made me ride a goat. I told her I couldn't tell her anything; she said, "You're just like your grandfather — he wouldn't tell me anything either."

Becoming a Mason was wonderful for me, because it restored my belief in the brotherhood of men. Somehow, sometime, somewhere during the war, I lost it. Words cannot describe the affect that combat has on sensitive people. To go out each day and let the enemy shoot at you and try to kill you, as you do your duties which may kill others, takes a lot more than courage. The enemy has to be defeated, and you have to be willing to die to accomplish this goal.

Captain Dick Crummett, taken December, 1945.

I'd forgotten home and family while I was over there. I felt out of place. Sort of like a stranger. I just didn't seem to fit into the family. I felt better if I was alone. I took walks down to the river and out in the woods. In December of 1945, I got orders to report to an Army base in Delaware, to be mustered out of the military. At this time, I signed up in the Air Force Reserve Corps as a Captain. Eventually, I got into the 512th Troop Carrier group, flying C-46's.

On my way back to Maine, I took a detour over to Reading, PA to see a girl I'd met back in '43. I'd met her when a plane load of us flew up to Reading to catch a train to Philadelphia to see the Army Navy football game; we missed the train. On our return, an oil pump failed on one of our engines shortly after we took off. We were stuck in Reading for a week until we got repaired. During that time I met this girl and her sister. They showed us where the clubs were, where we could enjoy music and dancing. She wrote to me while I was overseas.

Well, I called and her brother said okay to stop by—he'd tell her. I found their house all right. She was on her hands and knees scrubbing the kitchen floor. He'd forgotten to tell her I called. Was she surprised! Boy. She was beautiful. She was still the good girl I'd known before. I stayed in town a few days to get reacquainted and was favorably impressed. This girl had the character, morals and ideals of someone who'd make a man proud to have her as his wife.

I met men at the clubs and learned good jobs were available. The pay they were getting was better than anything in Maine. I'd not gotten interested in farming since my return. I went back home and thought things over. Finally told my dad, I didn't see any future in farming. He was disappointed, but wished me well as I left.

I came down to Reading again and finally talked my girl into marriage. We eloped down to Elkton, MD with two of her girlfriends as witnesses. I came home weary of the war; being sensitive, I carried a heavy load of memories and bad experiences. She helped me forget the war and got me back to being a normal person again.

I got a job right away and then a better one. I was a union worker, making good money. Finally had an accident whereby I got rolled up in a roll of fabric on a machine—amazingly, I survived. I soon realized I'd better go back to college and get my degree. I had two years of college when I enlisted in the Air Corps.

I got a B.A. degree at Colby College. My major was chemistry, in a pre-med course. I graduated in 1952 and went down to Temple University in Philadelphia and got accepted at their dental college. I couldn't come up with the money for tuition however so I got a job instead.

Soon, I got a better job as a safety man in a steel mill and later became a first aid instructor. I joined the fire brigade and soon became a certified fire fighter. I liked my steel mill job, but every spring they shut down for a few weeks to retool for the model changes. The union men were given a partial wage assistance, however as a company hourly man, I got nothing. Then, when I had to go for my weekend Air Force Reserve training, I'd have to get one of the other safety men to work my shift (the plant was in operation 24/7) and they did not pay me as they were supposed to.

Finally, on one of my layoffs, (I'd just brought my wife home from the hospital with our third child), I applied for a job as a safety advisor at an electronics manufacturer. I got hired and quit with the steel plant. This was challenging as most of the employees were women. I had to write monthly safety letters for the supervisors in the shop. I had to send in our safety statistics report to the National Safety Council. I got Top Secret security clearance, so I could show our engineers Top Secret films and slides. Ultimately, the company lost a government contract and I was laid off. I retired from the Air Force Reserve a Major, in 1962.

My wife Jane and I, around 1960. Taken at Newcastle, Delaware at a reunion for my 512th Troop Carrier Group.

I applied for a field engineer job with an insurance company and got hired. This entailed visiting locations to be insured, to get data and details via inspecting same, so the risks could be evaluated by the underwriters. This required writing detailed reports and scaled drawings with photos. This was challenging too, because they insured all kinds of mercantile, manufacturing, mining, healthcare, housing, hotels, municipal police and fire departments, summer youth camps, ski slopes, etc. If these locations had an elevator or a boiler, we inspected them also. Boy! Did I have to get books and study.

One of the men who was licensed by the state, started to teach me how to inspect elevators. With my high mechanical aptitude, it was easy. However, the state test requires you to draw or sketch certain critical safety components to show how they work. This was hard and took a lot of practice on each item so you could do it quickly and accurately.

I took the state test and passed on the first try. Few fellows do that. It took a full eight hours to complete the test. I enjoyed inspecting elevators. There are so many different kinds.

The older ones are sometimes unique. As time went by, eventually I left the insurance job, even after being certified as a professional safety engineer by the American Society of Safety Engineers.

My last job was with the Pennsylvania Department of Labor and Industry as an elevator inspector. I worked for them for ten years, and then retired. I made many friends over the years, and some enemies too—you get some of each if you do any job correctly and honestly. I've had a few accidents, injuries and close calls. But I'm happy. My guardian angel is still with me. Life's been good!

I joined the B-26 Marauder Historical Society as a life member a few years back. Soon, our 397th Bomb group started having reunions. In 1991, we had one in Baltimore. This was also to celebrate the 50th anniversary of the Martin B-26 marauder's production. I went and had a great time, but had so thoroughly wiped out memories of the war and our plane, that I couldn't recognize anybody or remember hardly anything. Before the reunion ended though, I'd kind of begun to recall some things, and got reacquainted with a couple of fellow pilots.Since then, I have spent my time trying to remember. It has been hard and painful at times, to recall things. If it hadn't been for some data I'd recorded in a little notebook, it would have been almost impossible.

A cartoon drawn by one of our retirees. Artist unknown.

Long ago, I wondered why my buddies, and not I, were killed. War is hell; ask any combat veteran. Of one thing I am sure; any one of us would've gladly given his life, to preserve America and her peoples' freedom and liberty. We all loved the U.S.A. We all had that sense of fidelity and moral duty to defend, protect and preserve America and our way of life.

As a pilot it was hard to be assigned as a co-pilot when I reported for duty with the 397th Bomb Group. However, I could see the big picture, and stoically accepted my assignment. I learned my duties quickly and performed them well; no doubt my pilot, Captain Don Stangle, helped my achievement tremendously.

Later, after 55 missions, as a first-pilot I would progress quite rapidly, due to my previous combat experience. I became an instrument flight-check pilot, a flight leader and then a squadron leader. Then I was a flight commander. I was promoted from 1st Lieutenant to Captain. From my notation in my little flight-diary of my flights, it seems that I may have flown 91 combat missions, at least.

My navigator told me after the war that my crew called me "Iron man," because I never showed any fear. This is probably true for the most part, but I was anxious on my first few missions. After being shot at and experiencing accurate flak, I accepted the fact that my fate no doubt lay in the hands of the Lord; I shouldn't have any fear. I had a job to do, flying, and getting my bombs on their target. One must concentrate and not be distracted by anything. That rule helped me to survive.

The End

AWARDS:

- Croix de Guerre with Silver Star
- Air Medal with 2 Silver and 2 Bronze Stars
- Presidential Unit Citation
- American Campaign Medal
- European, African, Middle-Eastern Campaign Medal with Six Clusters
- World War II Victory Medal

First Crew

April, 1944 – October, 1944

B-26 C296314U2V "Patty Kaye" (no nose art)

Pilot:Captain Donald Stangle (KIA)
Co-Pilot:Lt. Richard M. Crummett
Bombardier: Lt. Arthur Coyne
Navigator: Lt. Norman Scherer
Engineer/Tail Gunner:Sgt. Robert Adams
Top-Turret Gunner:Sgt. Robert Snow
Radio Man:Sgt. Perkins

Second Crew

December, 1944 – May, 1945*

B-26 G318096U2B "Massacre-Raiding Marauder"
Nose Art: Little Red Riding Hood's Wolf in Granny Cap

Pilot: 1st Lt. Richard M. Crummett
Co-Pilot:2nd Lt. James E. Voelker
Bombardier:2nd Lt. Frank Casella
Navigator:2nd Lt. Franklin Sanford
Engineer/Tail-Gunner: Sgt. Edward Yurkonis
Waist-Gunner/Radio-Man:Sgt. Norman Cole
Top-Turret Gunners:Sgt. Charles Hubach (KIA)
Sgt. Richard Humphries

* From October of 1944 through December of 1944, my crew was not fixed but varied for the most part. By December 15 of 1944, I believe I had a fixed crew.

Acknowledgment

I wish to thank and praise my oldest daughter, Cheryl Lynn Crummett, for her help, encouragement, suggestions and efforts to get me to produce a manuscript. Then she tirelessly tackled the proof-reading and editing of the book. I couldn't have done it without her.

Valhalla

The old Norse *warriors* believed that there was a place, Valhalla, to which they would all go when eventually they died or were killed, and I sometimes wonder, if maybe, *just maybe*, there's a special Valhalla just for flyers in general and Marauder men in particular?

If there is, then when we finally reach that wondrous place, we shall find, not only all our old comrades waiting for us, but also our old Marauders, standing in their dispersals, the summer sun glistening on cockpit, nose and turret plexiglas. Big Curtiss-Hamilton props all lined up, nose wheel straight, all damage patched and painted, bombed up, gassed up and ready to go once again.

Our aches and pains, the stiffening joints of age, are all gone. Wounds are healed, bodies are whole, we are all young again, and, as we assemble and listen to the familiar words of our briefing, the old feelings of excitement mingled with pride and tinged with apprehension come flooding back once more.

Briefing over, we spill out towards the waiting trucks, laughing, chattering, leg-pulling as always. Loading our gear, we climb aboard and set off toward the dispersal area, then crew by crew we drop off at our waiting aircraft.

External checks are completed, the entire crew: pilot, co-pilot, bombardier, navigator, gunners and radio operator climb aboard the plane. Up a ladder into the nose wheel well, through a hatch into the cockpit, we stow our gear and settle into our flight positions to begin the individual aircraft equipment checks.

Checks complete, we sit and wait, quiet now, as the minutes tick away towards start up time. As the second hand of every watch moves up to the appointed minute, the tension builds and then the whine as the engine starters engage, and one by one, left, then right, the big props begin to turn. A burst of smoke as each engine fires up, coughs and runs with that old familiar, thunderous roar, and every dispersal is echoing the same tune.

One more set of checks, bomb doors closed, brakes released, and we begin to ease out onto the taxiway, to join the long line of aircraft as they make their way towards the takeoff end of the strip.

In turn, each aircraft reaches the run-up point, turns into the wind, and powers up each engine, left, right, and then together. Finally, turn on the runway, full power, brakes off, they roll, slowly accelerating, on past the control tower until the rumble of the gear dies away and they are airborne, wheels up and climbing into that 10/10 blue sky once more.

The raid leader makes a wide turn, the formation assembles and we set course, climbing to operational height and the enemy ahead.

In this Valhalla, the strip is always long enough, there are no "runaway props", no burst tyres, no engine failures, and the flak (although it looks and sounds as menacing as ever) no longer maims and kills either aircraft or crew. The big R-2800's always run sweetly and unfalteringly, the fuel load is always ample for the mission, and the formations are wonderfully tight, but easily flown. Low cloud and fog are unknown, the sun shines from dawn to dusk, and the radio compass is tuned to where Dinah Shore is once more

singing all our old favorites, and we know, we surely know, that
We are home at last.

—Author Unknown

Captain Dick Crummett, in the cockpit.